GUY BEDOUELLE

The Reform of Catholicism, 1480–1620

Guy Bedouelle's *Reform of Catholicism, 1480–1620,* introduces nuances to earlier books on this subject by demonstrating how reform within the Roman Church owed much to a ferment and coordination of action emanating from its traditional geographic and jurisdictional centre, Rome. But, after showing how the Council of Trent legislated reform in the Church and empowered structures to carry it out, Bedouelle also highlights the actions of dedicated men and women that brought about a renewed spirit in the Church and in society – a "Catholicism" which, at least in some aspects, paralleled the way other Christians constituted a "Lutheranism," a "Calvinism," or an "Anglicanism."

> It is a long time since I have read a book in which the objectives are so clearly set out and concisely met. ... Within the space of just a few hours the reader has been provided with an impressively cogent *tour d'horizon* which has simply no rivals in what is now an increasingly crowded field. ... [It is] an excellent introduction to early modern Catholicism for undergraduates from departments of History, Theology, or Religious Studies [and] also plugs an important gap in the market for the interested layman.

> —SIMON DITCHFIELD, *University of York*

CATHOLIC AND RECUSANT TEXTS OF THE LATE MEDIEVAL & EARLY MODERN PERIODS

Edited by

T.S. FREEMAN, *University of Sheffield*

ANN M. HUTCHISON, *York University and PIMS*

ALISON SHELL, *University of Durham*

The Pontifical Institute of Mediaeval Studies acknowledges the generous assistance of JOSEPH and CLAUDINE POPE in the publication of Catholic and Recusant Texts of the Late Medieval and Early Modern Periods.

STUDIES AND TEXTS 161

GUY BEDOUELLE

The Reform of Catholicism, 1480–1620

Translated and annotated by

JAMES K. FARGE

PONTIFICAL INSTITUTE OF MEDIAEVAL STUDIES

Library and Archives Canada Cataloguing in Publication

Bedouelle, Guy
    The reform of Catholicism, 1480–1620 / Guy Bedouelle ; translated and annotated by James K. Farge.

(Catholic and recusant texts of the late medieval and early modern periods ; 1)
(Studies and texts, ISSN 0082–5328 ; 161)
Translation of La réforme du catholicisme (1480–1620).
Includes bibliographical references and index.

ISBN 978–0–88844–161–4

    1. Catholic Church – History – 16th century.   2. Counter-Reformation.
I. Farge, James K., 1938–   II. Pontifical Institute of Mediaeval Studies
III. Title.   IV. Series.   V. Series: Studies and texts (Pontifical Institute of Mediaeval Studies) ; 161

BR430.B4313 2008   270.6   C2008–906500–X

In memory of

Msgr Eugenio Corecco (1935–1995),

bishop of Lugano

Contents

Abbreviations

For publication details, please consult the bibliographies, pp. 137–51.

Canons and Decrees	*Canons and Decrees of the Council of Trent*, ed. and trans. Henry Joseph Schroeder
CT	*Concilium Tridentinum: diariorum, actorum, epistularum, tractatuum nova collectio*, ed. Societas Goerresiana
LW	*Luther's Works*, ed. Jaroslav Pelikan and Helmut T. Lehmann
Mansi	*Sacrorum conciliorum nova et amplissima collectio*, ed. Giovanni-Domenico Mansi et al.
Olin	*The Catholic Reformation: Savonarola to Ignatius Loyola; Reform in the Church, 1495–1540*, ed. John C. Olin
Tanner, *Decrees*	*Decrees of the Ecumenical Councils*, ed. Norman P. Tanner
WA	*D. Martin Luthers Werke: Kritische Gesamtausgabe* [Weimarer Ausgabe], ed. J.K.F. Knaake et al.

Translator's Note

The original French version of this book, *La réforme du catholicisme (1480–1620),* appeared in the series "Histoire du christianisme" (Paris: Cerf, 2002), of which the author is also the general editor. An Italian translation, *La riforma del cattolicesimo (1480–1620)* (Milan: Jaca Book), appeared in 2003, and a Spanish one – *La reforma del catolicismo (1480–1620)* (Madrid: Biblioteca de Autores Cristianos) – in 2005. In it Guy Bedouelle provides a general synthesis of the movement of Church reform in the sixteenth century and presents his personal interpretation of its vicissitudes, successes, and significance. While Professor Bedouelle recognizes the validity of the terminology that other historians have applied to the reform movement and of the approaches to it and interpretations of it that they have put forward, he proposes that the ideas, agenda, and actions of the Catholic Church in the sixteenth century are best conveyed by the title he has chosen for the book: *The Reform of Catholicism.*

The French, Italian, and Spanish versions of this book appeared in series that were primarily directed at a general readership. As such, they provided no footnotes or annotation, although some minimal documentation was inserted into the text itself. The sources consulted by the author were listed in the Essential Bibliography, which was then divided into two sections – one on the concept of Catholic reform, the other on its history.

This English translation is aimed at a wider audience that will include not only the general reader but also students in the classroom and others who may want to research particular points more thoroughly. For this reason, I have opted to provide footnote references with detailed documentation of the sources on which the text relies. When possible, English-language sources, both primary and secondary, have also been provided. In the footnotes and in constructing the Bibliography, I have placed in the short Select Bibliography the sources which most prominently served both Guy Bedouelle and me. All other sources consulted, as well as some of the other sources available in English, are listed in the General Bibliography. Any

errors or omissions in the footnotes and bibliographies are attrib-
utable to me alone, not to Professor Bedouelle.

It has been both a privilege and an education for me to translate
this work composed by a distinguished author whose more than
twenty published books cover a wide range of subjects in early modern and modern religious history.

James K. Farge, CSB
Pontifical Institute of Mediaeval Studies

Preface to the English Edition

The period stretching from the end of the fifteenth century to the beginning of the seventeenth – roughly, 1480 to 1620 – left its mark on the history of the West in a number of fundamental ways. In regard to the Catholic church, that era produced an ecclesiastical order, doctrinal interpretations, and disciplinary norms which held sway in the Church right up to the Second Vatican Council in the mid-twentieth century.

This reform within the Roman Church has been widely – and often very well – studied. The terms which different historians have chosen to sum up its impact on history usually reveal the particular angle or position from which they have viewed it. Early on, they tended to refer to it as "the Counter-Reformation," thus choosing to regard Catholic reform primarily as a reaction to "the Reformation" (which required no further modifier as "Protestant"). Somewhat later, some historians realized it was necessary to speak of "the Catholic Reformation" in order to take into account the many vital reform measures undertaken in the fifteenth and early sixteenth century – initiatives prior to and quite independent of Protestantism. This was a time when historians began to profit from methodologies employed by other sciences, such as sociology, in order to discover and appreciate the lively piety and commitment of the people of God in the "pre-Reformation" years.

The present book has no wish to deny or supplant the importance of those two approaches: the Catholic reaction to Protestantism ("Counter-Reformation") and the concrete, collective life of the Catholic people ("Catholic Reformation"). But it does, however, propose to introduce a supplementary nuance to those interpretations. Quite simply, it describes how the reform within the Roman Church was achieved by an initial ferment and a later coordination of endeavours emanating from its traditional geographic and jurisdictional centre. The book goes into some detail to describe how the Council of Trent played a strategic role in legislating reform in the Church and how it empowered structures to carry it out. At the same time, however, the book also maintains that none of that would have been effective without a renewed spirit at all levels of society and without the dedicated action of men and women – some famous, others anonymous – who were agents of the reform both prior to and after the Council.

Taking this approach also enables us better to understand how, starting in the decades between 1530 and 1560, the belief and practice of Catholics came to constitute a "Catholicism" – much in the way that other Christians yearning for reform constituted a "Lutheranism," a "Calvinism," or an "Anglicanism." Recent historiography underlines this ecclesiastical phenomenon of "confessionalization." The thesis of this book and the title I have given it – "The Reform of Catholicism" – maintains that, as part of any interpretation of the wide range of global history, we should not fail to acknowledge the strategic role of the ecclesiastical institution which inspired the groups and individuals acting under its aegis.

Admittedly limited in scope by its brevity, this book owes much, at several stages of its preparation, to others. I am grateful, first of all, to my students at the Université de Fribourg in Switzerland and then, at a second stage, to a group of young historian friends. As well, the present book has profited from the reactions and remarks of several authors of reviews of the original French version and of the manuscript of this English one. But this book would not be what it has become – with its added complement of footnote references, annotations, extended bibliographies, and indexes – without the painstaking work of James K. Farge, whose works on the religious and intellectual scene in early sixteenth-century France are well known. He has produced a remarkably fluent English translation and, in using his historian's insight, has posed questions which have enabled me to introduce a number of precisions and clarifications into this English edition. I extend here my heartfelt gratitude to him. Together we hope this book will serve well those who seek to know more about this strategic era in the history of Christianity.

Guy Bedouelle, OP
Rector, Université catholique de l'Ouest (Angers, France)
Feast of St Ignatius of Loyola, 31 July 2008

Introduction

The historical problem that concerns us here is a simple one: why did reform of the Catholic Church – something that was ardently desired by many and attempted several times before and after the fourteenth century – have to wait until the end of the sixteenth century, and in some ways until the seventeenth, to take hold firmly in the Church? Put another way: why was the Council of Trent able to accomplish successfully what the wishes and efforts of earlier councils, popes, and saints – from Catherine of Siena to Vincent Ferrer and Savonarola – had failed to do?

The answer to that clear, but not very simple, question is deeply enmeshed in the complexities of the waning Middle Ages and of the unfolding Renaissance. This difficulty is borne out by the numerous historical explanations, many of which, time and again, have been proposed on behalf of deep-seated confessional considerations and which seem even to have multiplied in recent years. As we attempt to ferret out our answer we cannot avoid those underlying, sometimes problematic matters.

It should be clear from the beginning, however, that this book is not intended to be a "history of the Reformation." It lies beyond our scope here to emulate or summarize the many solid studies of the Protestant Reformation and its leading personalities that have appeared in recent decades. Rather, it is our intention to examine the ideas about, and the movement towards, reform within the Roman Catholic Church – or, as our title suggests, within "Catholicism."

Let us begin by evoking some of those ideas, movements, and problematic matters. First of all, we shall examine the vocabulary that historians of the Reformation era have used ever since the eighteenth century. Their words and expressions have long been the subject of dispute, of doubts, and of redefinition. Our starting point in this quest will be borrowed from the text written by Msgr Hubert Jedin on the occasion of the fourth centenary of the opening of the Council of

Trent.[1] This short but momentous book went largely unnoticed when it was published, but it has since been translated into English[2] – but not French – and is even now in its fifth Italian edition.[3] It remains an essential component of the historiography of the sixteenth century. We shall borrow freely from it as we examine the vocabulary and the underlying themes of reform and reformation as proposed, demanded, and expounded in discourses pronounced and texts written in the fifteenth and sixteenth centuries.

We shall also, of course, examine some representative positions of and texts written by Protestant Reformers, so that we may attempt to understand precisely what they meant when they demanded that the Church of which they were members be "reformed." In this we shall observe that their original intentions and conception of reform changed over time. As well, we must explore the common historiographical thesis which sees the emergence of Protestantism as the principal motivation behind Catholic reform. In other words, would there have been a reform of Catholicism in Europe without the Protestant Reformation? Is such a position valid; and, if it is, to what extent?

To avoid having to narrate all the ups and downs of four centuries of Church history, however, we shall for the most part limit ourselves to the sixteenth century, for which the bibliography is already so rich. Still, because events and periods of history cannot be limited by the round numbers of a century's opening and closing, we shall sometimes pursue our investigations into the period prior to 1500 and into the 1620s as well.

Another question which concerns us is this: why was the Council of Trent able to succeed in its goal of renewing the western Catholic Church – and, indeed, renewing it even more successfully than one

1 Jedin, *Katholische Reformation oder Gegenreformation? Ein Versuch zur Klärung der Begriffe nebst einer Jubiläumsbetrachtung über das Trienter Konzil* (Lucerne, 1946).
2 Jedin, *Catholic Reformation or Counter-Reformation?* trans. David M. Luebke, in *The Counter-Reformation: The Essential Readings,* ed. David M. Luebke (Oxford; Malden, Mass., 1999), 9–46.
3 Jedin, *Riforma cattolica o Controriforma? Tentativo di chiarimento dei concetti con riflessioni sul Concilio di Trento,* trans. Marola Guarducci (Brescia, 1995). The first Italian edition was published in 1957.

could have hoped? Developing answers to all these questions will allow us, we hope, to provide the reader with a *status quaestionis* which will highlight, for this period in the history of the Church, what amounted to a confrontation of Catholicism with the modern world.

This book is divided into twelve chapters and a conclusion. After examining the origin of the concepts and the terminology used by historians, it examines the goals of the councils, especially Lateran V. It then turns its attention to the Protestant Reformers, whose very name indicates their ambition, demands for, and claims of reform. At the same time we shall see that there were parallel proposals and even precise, courageous innovations within the traditional Church which would serve as a framework for eventual reform. The Council of Trent found itself in a climate that was saturated with ideas and initiatives for reform, each of which inevitably raised political and ecclesiastical hackles; but it managed in the end to find and act upon a vision that held in balance tradition, doctrine, and a reformation of discipline in such a way as to implement an effective Catholic reformation.

The structure of the book and the series which it joins are designed to present the reader with a somewhat general and wide-ranging synthesis, although it will be substantiated by precise examples intended to justify it and flesh it out. The bibliography is likewise restricted to works cited and to other works which will aid the readers to develop further what they have read and to help them reflect on this fascinating history of a century that is a turning point in the history of Christianity.

The city of Fribourg, Switzerland, where I taught for nearly thirty years, has long been recognized as a place which typifies the reform of Catholicism in the early modern period – a reform that so many longed for and that others have affirmed over the centuries. Its Jesuit school and baroque church where Saint Peter Canisius is buried; its Capuchin monastery, its cloister of Visitation nuns and its Ursuline schools; its seminaries (founded somewhat later); its solemn feast of Corpus Christi, when the streets host a long procession led by Swiss Guards accompanying city officials, clergy, and the bishop bearing the monstrance holding the Holy Eucharist towards a covered altar of repose – all bear witness to the Catholic mind-set fashioned in the sixteenth through the nineteenth centuries and carried on even today.

CHAPTER ONE

Words Historians Use

When historians set out to describe their research and its results, they must use categories and concepts. Some of these they discovered in reading other historians, and others they invented while interpreting their own research. In order to communicate those concepts to their colleagues and to the public, they must employ a vocabulary that their readers can accept and understand, and they must take care that the terminology they use is appropriate to the period of history they are attempting to describe.

Intelligible historical discourse also calls for a certain classification or division of the past into periods of time. Although the flow of time in itself is obviously uninterrupted, historians resort to chronological subdivisions within the passage of time. For example, when Jacques Heers[1] wanted to describe the fourteenth and fifteenth centuries, he called them "transitional times."

The object of our reflection here is "Reform." Gerhart B. Ladner[2] has shown that the term "Reform" (whether capitalized or not) can be applied to every period in the history of the Church since its earliest centuries. The word is most commonly used, however, to designate two precise periods or movements within western religious history: the "Gregorian Reform" in the eleventh and twelfth centuries and what we tend to call "the Reformation" (with a capital R) to designate the beginning and development of Protestantism in the sixteenth century. If today you use the word "Reformation" in a conversation about history, those who hear you or read you will presume that you are speaking or writing about the second of these, the Protestant Reformation in the sixteenth century.

---

1   Heers, *Le Moyen âge, une imposture* (Paris, 1992).
2   Ladner, *The Idea of Reform: Its Impact on Christian Thought and Action in the Age of the Fathers* (Cambridge, Mass., 1959).

This quasi-monopoly of the concept of reformation as pertaining to Protestantism has been strengthened by the creation of another concept – the "Counter-Reformation" – to designate a defensive reaction on the part of Catholicism. In this chapter, as we attempt to query the historiographical record of this range of vocabulary, we will often draw upon Hubert Jedin[3] and also on a more recent author, John W. O'Malley.[4]

The origin of the term "Counter-Reformation" can be attributed to Johann Pötter (†1807), a jurist of Göttingen. He used the word *Gegenreformation* as early as 1776 to designate the return to Catholicism of German territories that had earlier embraced Protestantism. For him, therefore, the meaning of the term was limited both by geography and by a specific period of time. A century later, the great German historian Leopold von Ranke (†1886) appropriated that meaning in a wider, if more nuanced, historiographical usage. Still later, Moriz Ritter[5] (†1923), a Bonn professor and adherent of the Old Catholic Church, popularized Pötter's term "Counter-Reformation" and extended it beyond the geographical confines of Germany. When Eberhard Gothein wrote in 1895 about Ignatius of Loyola, he adopted Ritter's geographical extension of the term but used it in a wider sense to describe a return to a medieval spirituality.

Other German historians did not hesitate to follow this historiographical trend. Ludwig von Pastor (†1928), in his monumental *History of the Popes*,[6] and Johann Schmidlin (†1944), who substituted the term "Catholic Restoration," both accepted the idea that the Catholic Church reacted in shock to Protestantism, but they modified

3   See the Introduction, nn1–3.
4   O'Malley, ed., *Catholicism in Early Modern History: A Guide to Research* (St Louis, Mo., 1988).
5   Ritter, *Deutsche Geschichte im Zeitalter der Gegenreformation und des dreissigjährigen Krieges (1555–1648)* (Stuttgart, 1889–1908; 2nd ed. Darmstadt, 1962).
6   Pastor, *The History of the Popes: from the Close of the Middle Ages, Drawn from the Secret Archives of the Vatican and other Original Sources,* ed. and trans. F.I. Antrobus et al. (London; St Louis, Mo., 1891–1961). Originally published as *Geschichte der Päpste seit dem Ausgang des Mittelalters mit Benutzung des Päpstlichen Geheimarchives und vieler andere Archive* (Freiburg-im-Breisgau, 1886–1933).

its use to parallel a Restoration of a monarchy, such as occurs after a political Revolution has played itself out. This term "Catholic Restoration" was adopted in 1960 for the title of one of the volumes in the French collection *Histoire de l'Église* known commonly by the name of its editors, "Fliche et Martin."

In the end, many historians preferred and adopted an alternate term: "Catholic Reform." It was popularized, if not invented, by the Protestant historian Wilhelm Maurenbrecher[7] (†1930), who preferred it to the term "Counter-Reformation" which Ranke had used and to that of "Roman Reform" which still others had proposed.

It is quite clear, then, that the terminology about Church reform and the debates that accompanied its use first emerged from German historiographical usage. It was a milieu in which confessional options often played a role – and much of it took place in the midst of the *Kulturkampf*, in which some German historians were quite willing to view Tridentine Catholicism as nothing more than an anti-Protestant strategy.

Still, the term "Counter-Reformation" has been widely used and accepted by many Catholic historians and has made its way into other historiographical traditions. In the English language the use of "Counter-Reformation" is common enough. In France, Augustin Renaudet's remarkable thesis[8] devised a simple and simplifying historical sequence: the Protestant Reformation was anticipated by a "Pre-Reformation" of an evangelical type and was followed, in reaction, by a Counter-Reformation instigated by the Roman Church. About the same time, the monumental work by the Catholic historian Pierre Imbart de La Tour,[9] without proposing an alternative terminology, supplied a number of useful elements that helped to nuance Renaudet's notion of "Pre-Reformation."

Many authors have sensed that these concepts were too uniform. One of these was Ludwig von Pastor[10] as he produced volume after

---

7   Maurenbrecher, preface to *Geschichte der katholischen Reformation* (Nördlingen, 1880).
8   Renaudet, *Préréforme et humanisme à Paris pendant les premières guerres d'Italie (1494–1517)* (Paris, 1916; 2nd ed. 1953).
9   Imbart de La Tour, *Les origines de la Réforme* (Paris, 1905–1935).
10 See n6 above.

volume of his *History of the Popes* up to the year of his death. Others, in treating particular episodes of the religious history of the sixteenth century, were able to make the idea of "Catholic Reform" a familiar and acceptable one. Victor Martin, as we mentioned above, used it in the title of one of his books.[11]

The second half of the twentieth century has seen a continued tendency to nuance and to juxtapose these concepts without renouncing them outright. Already in 1929 Lucien Febvre[12] did not hesitate to challenge in an iconoclastic fashion not only the terminology but also the concepts commonly used by historians. In the conclusion of his 1946 article on Bishop Guillaume Briçonnet, Febvre situated his subject in

> a time when the destinies of Reformation and Counter-Reformation – if we can indeed continue to use those terms – were not yet dissociated. But would it not be better to renounce once and for all those misleading labels: Pre-Reformation, Reformation, and Counter-Reformation? Personally, I would rather speak of Renovations, Revolutions, Revisions – three steps in one same religious movement which surpasses the concept of Reformation while, at the same time, encompasses it without being absorbed in it to such an extent that the vocabulary suppresses everything that it cannot include.[13]

Like so many of the authors that we have cited, Hubert Jedin (†1980) accepts and utilizes both terms, "Catholic Reform" and "Counter-Reformation," in his magisterial work on the Council of

---

11   Martin, *Le Gallicanisme et la réforme catholique; essai historique sur l'introduction en France des décrets du Concile de Trente (1563–1615)* (Paris, 1919).

12   Febvre, "The Origins of the French Reformation: A Badly-put Question?" trans. K. Folka, in *A New Kind of History, from the Writings of Lucien Febvre*, ed. Peter Burke (New York; Evanston, Ill., 1973), 44–107. Originally published as "Une question mal posée: les origines de la Réforme française et le problème des causes de la Réforme," in *Revue Historique* 159 (1929): 1–73; repr. in *Au coeur religieux du XVIe siècle* (Paris, 1957; 2nd ed. 1968; repr. 1983), 3–70.

13   Febvre, "Idée d'une recherche d'histoire comparée: Le cas Briçonnet," *Annuaire de l'École pratique des Hautes Études* (Paris, 1946), repr. in *Au coeur religieux du XVIe siècle* (Paris, 1957; 2nd ed. 1968; repr. 1983), 161.

Trent,[14] in his book on Cardinal Girolamo Seripando,[15] one of the leading figures at Trent, and in the series of Reformation-era Catholic authors he has edited.[16] For him the term "Catholic Reform," like that of *Selbstbesinnung* (a realization by the Catholic Church of what she is) comprised several phases. The first phase, at the end of the Middle Ages, had its roots in the *devotio moderna* and in the return of the religious orders to a stricter observance of their monastic Rule. A second phase, beginning about 1540, was linked to the foundation of the Jesuits and the strengthening of the reformist aspirations of the papacy. The third coincided with the opening of the Council of Trent. The fourth, beginning with the application of the Council's decisions, extended into the decades and the century after the Council. The Counter-Reformation, for Jedin, was a question of self-defense (*Selbstbehauptung*) that began in 1520 with the controversies against Luther, with the creation of the Roman Inquisition in 1542, and with the development of the Index of Prohibited Books.

As one might expect it was in Italy where the debate about revising the traditional terminology occurred first and where it had the greatest repercussions. Paradoxically, the distinction was strongly accepted and employed by the historian of Italian heretics Delio Cantimori (†1966),[17] and it was supported and developed by a disciple of Jedin, Paolo Prodi.[18] Contrary to them, Sergio Zoli – and even more

14 Jedin, *A History of the Council of Trent,* trans. Ernest Graf (London, 1957). Only the first two volumes of the German text, *Geschichte des Konzils von Trient* (Freiburg, 1949), have been translated.

15 Jedin, *Papal legate at the Council of Trent, Cardinal Seripando*, trans. Frederic C. Eckhoff (St Louis, Mo., 1957). Originally published as *Girolamo Seripando: Sein Leben und Denken im Geisteskampf des 16. Jahrhunderts* (Würzburg, 1937; repr. Würzburg, 1984).

16 The series *Corpus Catholicorum* was conceived as a collection of writings by the leading sixteenth-century proponents of Roman Catholicism defending the doctrines of the Catholic Church against the teachings of the Protestant reformers. It includes 48 volumes published from 1919 to the present.

17 Cantimori, *Eretici italiani del Cinquecento e altri scritti*, ed. Adriano Prosperi (Turin, 1992); cf. *Eretici italiani del Cinquecento e Prospettive di storia ereticale italiana del Cinquecento*, ed. A. Prosperi (Turin, 2002).

18 Prodi, "Controriforma e/o riforma cattolica: Superamento di vecchi dilemmi nei nuovi panorami storiografici," *Römische historische Mitteilungen* 31 (1989): 227–37.

Paolo Simoncelli in his study of Italian Spirituals – have actively challenged the use of the concept of "Catholic Reform."[19] They hold that the term Counter-Reformation quite aptly describes what happened in the Catholic Church in the sixteenth century. Their discussion has therefore taken place, whether openly or tacitly, in the acrimony that sometimes exists between lay and clerical approaches to history in twentieth-century Italy.

While continuing to hold to Jedin's two-term synthesis, as he calls it, Prodi later proposed that it was time to go beyond it and to see history in a more complex way (1989). At the same time, Giuseppe Alberigo pointed out the poverty of putting too much stress on the two terms. He felt it was necessary to adopt a more inclusive and rich historiography, especially when approaching spirituality and piety. This is best shown in the works of Giuseppe De Luca and Gabriele De Rosa and in the "history of mentalities" approach advanced by the French *Annales* school.

In Germany, as well, Jedin's two-term synthesis received both acceptance and criticism. In 1976, for example, Gottfried Maron criticized the concept of Catholic Reform for putting too much stress on continuity while minimizing the profound changes which took place in the sixteenth century.

If Marc Venard was correct to write in 1977[20] of a "confusion" in the vocabulary, it is worth noting that other prominent French historians of the sixteenth century, such as Jean Delumeau and Pierre Chaunu, have tended to use, conjointly and in the plural sense, the two traditional terms. For this reason, Bernard Roussel and I chose as the title for our collective work on the Bible in the sixteenth century *Le temps des Réformes et la Bible.*[21]

---

19   See Zoli, *Europa libertina tra controriforma e illuminismo: L' "Oriente" dei libertini e le origini dell'Illuminismo: studi e ricerche* (Bologna, 1989); see also Simoncelli, *Evangelismo italiano del Cinquecento: Questione religiosa e nicodemismo politico* (Rome, 1979).

20   Venard, "Réforme, Réformation, Préréforme, Contre-Réforme ... Étude de vocabulaire chez les historiens récents de langue française," in *Historiographie de la Réforme*, ed. Philippe Joutard (Neuchâtel; Paris, 1977); repr. in his *Le catholicisme à l'épreuve dans la France du XVIe siècle* (Paris, 2000), 1–26.

21   (Paris, 1989). This is volume 5 of *La Bible de tous les temps.*

Venard opted to entitle his 1992 book *The Time of Confessional-ization*.[22] This idea had already been utilized in Germany by Ernst Walter Zeeden in 1958 and then systematized by Wolfgang Reinhard[23] and Heinz Schilling in the 1980s. In 1981, writing about German and Swiss history, Bernd Vogler developed this approach further. He rightly noted that the most significant phenomenon of the sixteenth century was the development of different confessional Churches. One can in fact discern the constitution of new Churches which themselves rest on dogmatic consolidation. The first manifestations of this were given at the express order of Emperor Charles V in the statements of faith that different representatives presented at the Diet of Augsburg in 1530, of which the most famous and long-lasting was precisely the famous "Confession of Augsburg."[24] This was followed later by the "Confession of La Rochelle" in France (1559) and the "Formula of Concord" (1577) that was drawn up for German principalities and cities. This strengthening of the Catholic confessional base was to be provided by the doctrines and decrees of the Council of Trent which were diffused and popularized to a certain degree by confessional documents like the Profession of Faith of Pius IV or, more impor-tantly, the Roman Catechism. From this point of view we can better understand the significance of the principle *"cujus regio, ejus religio"* which gave a political and territorial foundation to confessionalism.

In his recent interpretive work, when speaking of the Catholic Church, Marc Venard underlines how it differed in the sixteenth cen-tury from medieval Christianity:

22 Venard, *Le temps des confessions (1530–1620/30)*, vol. 8 of *Histoire du chris-tianisme des origines à nos jours*, ed. Jean-Marie Mayeur (Paris, 1992). The series comprises 14 volumes.

23 Reinhard, "Pressures towards Confessionalization? Prolegomena to a Theory of the Confessional Age," in C. Scott Dixon, ed., *The German Reformation: The Essential Readings* (Oxford; Malden, Mass., 1999), 169–92. Originally pub-lished as "Zwang zur Konfessionalisierung? Prolegomena zu einer Theorie des konfessionellen Zeitalters," *Zeitschrift für Historische Forschung* 10 (1983): 257–77.

24 *The Book of Concord: The Confessions of the Evangelical Lutheran Church*, ed. Robert Kolb and Timothy Wengert, trans. Charles Arand et al. (Minneapolis, 2000), 27–105, gives English translations of both the original German and Latin texts of the Augsburg Confession.

Historians have debated extensively the meaning of this mutation, and their own point of view can be discerned in the titles they give to this historical movement: will it be "Counter-Reformation" or "Catholic Reform"? If one sees that the roots of Catholic reform delve as deeply as those of Protestantism in the reformist zeal of the late Middle Ages and owe nothing to Luther, one opts for "Catholic Reform." But if one considers that the pressure of the Reformers' revolutionary actions and of the dividing of Christianity were essential elements in bringing about reform, and that the definition of Catholic dogmas was done precisely to respond to Protestantism even at the risk of widening the division, one must opt for "Counter-Reformation."[25]

The logic of this distinction that Venard had already proposed in 1977 can hardly be denied. But should we not make clear as well that one makes such distinctions in order to unite the two concepts, "Counter-Reformation" and "Catholic Reform," again into one synthesis? In fact, they are not exclusive, and historians must recognize that each has legitimacy and must ponder the importance of both. This is what we shall attempt to do in the pages that follow.

The discussion is far from over. In France, the works of Thierry Wanegffelen invite us to think "outside the confessional model" in order to take into account those men in the sixteenth century who found themselves caught between the two sides (*entre deux chaires*).[26] Marc Venard, Alain Tallon, and others continue the debate. Recent works published in the United States avoid both terms in favour of taking a longer view. Thus Ronald Po-chia Hsia speaks of Catholic "renewal," placing the accent on *renovatio* rather than on *reformatio*,[27] while Robert Bireley both enlarges and maintains the debate by mixing the old and the new. He chose as his title: *The Refashioning of Catholicism, 1450–1700*, but he adds as a sub-title: *A Reassessment of the Counter Reformation*.[28]

25 Venard, *Le temps des confessions (1530–1620/30)*, 223.
26 Wanegffelen, *Une difficile fidélité: Catholiques malgré le concile en France, XVIe–XVIIe siècles* (Paris, 1999).
27 Hsia, *The World of Catholic Renewal, 1540–1770* (Cambridge, 1998; 2nd ed. 2005).
28 (Washington, D.C., 1999).

John O'Malley has proposed using a new, all-embracing term: "Early Modern Catholicism"; but he has also cautioned that "we ought to accept the multiplicity of terms," that "the search for a perfect designation is futile," and that "I have always insisted that [the term "Early Modern Catholicism"] was meant not to replace the other terms but to complement them."[29] We ought to look not to create diversity among ourselves about categories or expressions but to see what the historian can help us recover from the past. One of the most penetrating, elegant, and synthetic texts on this subject was composed in 1951 for the Bierbeck Lectures at Cambridge University by the English historian Henry Outram Evennett (†1964), who gave it the title *The Spirit of the Counter-Reformation*.[30] Wolfgang Reinhard has justly concluded that, in describing the Counter-Reformation as "an updating, a new *modus vivendi* [of the Catholic Church] with the world," Evennett went to the heart of the matter.

The title of the present work makes no claim to nullify or supersede the terminological debates we have described above. But it does adhere to the word "Reform" for several reasons. Aside from the fact that it would be hard to neglect this word which has been prominent in the historiography about the Church for several centuries, its use is consonant with the principal thesis of this book: that the joint, complementary consideration and articulation of the dogmatic and disciplinary decrees in the *De reformatione* of Trent is the key to its lasting success.

This thesis in no way tries to exclude other interpretations of this watershed period in the history of the Catholic Church. Nor does it pretend to be an all-inclusive presentation of Catholic attitudes of that time. In giving a prominent place to the Council of Trent and in analyzing closely the way it dealt with dogma and discipline, there is no intention to present here a kind of "official history" that would overshadow the importance of previous or parallel efforts that worked

---

29 O'Malley, *Trent and All That: Renaming Catholicism in the Early Modern Era* (Cambridge, Mass., 2000), especially the Conclusion: "There's Much in a Name," 119–43.

30 Published posthumously by John Bossy (Cambridge, 1968; repr. Notre Dame, Ind., 1970, 1975).

for Catholic reform. We have, however, wanted to show how the phenomenon of confessionalization that took place in all the Churches in the second half of the sixteenth century – and which has been highlighted by recent historiography – manifested itself quite strongly in the soul-searching that took place at the Council of Trent. Confessionalization took root and flourished in Catholicism because the Roman Church consciously and vigorously took up the will to reform itelf. At Trent it adopted an intelligent formula for achieving reform and set in motion measures that would carry it out.

"Reform" is a word which, through centuries of Church history, has been constantly present in all efforts of renewal and restoration. As we approach this study of it, we are conscious of the fact that in our own time Yves Congar invited us to discern between "true and false reform of the Church."[31] His was indeed a challenge which anticipated the Second Vatican Council and looked forward to a new *modus vivendi* of the Church with the world.

31 Congar, *Vraie et fausse réforme dans l'Église* (Paris, 1950; 2nd ed. 1968).

CHAPTER TWO

Yearning for Reform

Appeals for reform in the Church were made throughout the Middle Ages, and many of them were answered. The limited scope of this book precludes mentioning more than a few of them. The achievements of the "Gregorian Reform" at the end of the eleventh century had reached their apogee at the end of the twelfth and during the thirteenth century. Towards the end of that century Pope Boniface VIII, following in the tradition of strong popes from Gregory VII, Innocent III, and Gregory IX, tried to restrain the attempts of King Philip IV to control the Church in France. Boniface's bull *Unam Sanctam* (1302) set forth his ideas about papal sovereignty, but it served only to exacerbate the troubles for the papacy in the first years of the fourteenth century. Ridiculed and even physically manhandled, Boniface died in humiliating defeat. For nearly a century after that, the popes lived in exile in Avignon, where their independence vis-à-vis the French monarchy, even in purely Church matters, was precarious and, in the eyes of many, seriously compromised.

It was in the beginning of that weakened state of the papacy that Pope Clement V convened the Council of Vienne. The bull *Regnans in excelsis*[1] of 12 August 1308 demanded that he be informed about "everything that requires revision or correction."[2] He called for "an examination of conscience of Christendom." In answer to his demands, letters of complaint and accusation found their way to Vienne in 1309. The suggestions of Guillaume Durant the Younger, bishop of Mende (1296–1330), reflecting the thoughts of his more famous predecessor and namesake, helped set the agenda for reform which was to resound through the next four centuries. The Church, he said, must be reformed at two levels, in its hierarchy and in the people, in its

---

1   Giovanni-Domenico Mansi, Philippe Labbé, et al., eds. *Sacrorum conciliorum nova et amplissima collectio* ... (Florence; Venice, 1758–1799; repr. Paris; Leipzig; Arnhem, 1903–1927), 25: 369–88. (= Mansi.)
2   "quae correctionis et reformationis limam exposcunt." Mansi 25: 374E.

clergy and its laity. He used the celebrated formula: reform the Church *tam in capite quam in membris* – in its head and in its members.[3]

By reform of the "head" of the Church Durant unequivocally meant the papacy and the papal court. Only if they reformed themselves could they incite others – bishops, clerics, and lay people – to reform themselves in turn. No prince, no pope is above the law. Popes can decide nothing which is contrary to the decrees of councils and of the common law. Durant's words would be taken up again by Gallican theologians in the seventeenth century, but he was not what would later be termed a "conciliarist." He was simply a jurist expressing his views at the height of a crisis. He above all wanted to strengthen the Church in its struggle against a world constantly attracted by values other than those of the Gospel. To proclaim the Gospel in season and out of season, he said, the Church must constantly be reformed.

We know that one of the most serious crises in the history of the Church began in 1378 after Pope Gregory XI moved the papacy from Avignon back to Rome. This led to the Great Western Schism in which two and, later, three men claimed to be the one true pope, thus dividing the Latin Church and Latin Christendom during nearly forty years. It is in this context that we now evoke another call for reform: that by a Dominican tertiary, St Catherine of Siena. Although Catherine was absolutely committed to the legitimacy of the Roman pope, she was equally convinced that the Church – which she calls "the Mystical Body of Christ" – had to be reformed. In her efforts to reform the Dominican Order she worked through her disciple, Raymond of Capua. In regard to the Church in general her lamentations are eloquent testimony to her sincere distress over its hierarchy and its people. Her *Dialogue*, a series of conversations with God, has God depicting the Church as a woman whose face is so besmirched that anyone seeing her would think her a leper, her breasts swollen "because of the pride and avarice of ... my ministers who feed at her breasts"; but she later describes God's desire to wash the face of his

3 Guillaume Durant the Younger wrote *Tractatus de modo generalis concilii cele-brandi*. On him see Joseph Lecler, SJ, *Histoire des conciles oecuméniques* vol. 8: *Vienne* (Paris, 1964), 38–50.

Bride, to reform the Church.[4] Still later, God confides to her: "Now listen well, dearest daughter ... no matter where you turn, to secular or religious, clerics or prelates, lowly or great, young or old, you see nothing but sin." On the subject of prelates, she is told that "bloated with pride as they are, they never have their fill of gobbling up earthly riches and the pleasures of the world, while they are stingy, greedy, and avaricious toward the poor."[5] Her divine interlocutor promises to answer her prayers by bringing an end to the Schism. He tells her that she herself will not see it happen, because she has been invited by God "to reform the Church with her sweet, loving, and sorrowful desires, with her tears, and with her humble, continual prayer," and has thus figuratively sacrificed her life for the Church that she loves.[6]

In these two examples of reform – the Council of Vienne and the role of St Catherine of Siena – we see two traditional but distinct approaches to reform in the Church. The first is the institutional way, usually by way of a council; the second is the mystical way, the way of prayer, sanctity, and sacrifice. Both ways continued to be invoked in the fifteenth century. To both ways would be added new elements or examples.

The Council of Constance (1414–1418) restored the seamless robe of the Latin Church that had been rent asunder by the Great Schism, but its success was tinged with the hue of conciliarism which taught that councils had greater authority than the pope. All through the fifteenth century conciliarism continued to present itself as a rival of the papacy – most notably at the Council of Basel (1431–1449). Should ecclesiological conflict of this kind continue, it would surely make the possibility of reform by way of a council more risky and thus less likely to be tried by future popes.

The second way of reform, the mystical way, was tried, for example, at the end of the century by Girolamo Savonarola. After successfully reforming his priory of San Marco in Florence, he arrived at some reform of the morals in the city of Florence. He hoped to extend

4   Catherine of Siena, *The Dialogue*, trans. Suzanne Noffke, OP (New York, 1990), 50, 54.
5   Catherine of Siena, *The Dialogue*, trans. Noffke, 231, 232.
6   Catherine of Siena, *The Dialogue*, trans. Noffke, 51–3.

this to Tuscany, to all of Italy and Rome, and finally to the whole Church. This all-enveloping desire for reform had been aroused in Savonarola by the obvious incapacity of the papacy of the Borgia Pope Alexander VI to reform itself or any other part of the Church. Over-reaching himself, Savonarola's reform efforts were too mixed up with political contingencies and with an apocalyptic vision of an earthly kingdom of Christ. Nevertheless, his influence would be felt long after his execution at the hands of his enemies.

From that time on, although the idea of reform was never absent from the thoughts of many figures in the Church, it was hindered by hesitations arising from fear of repeating precedents that were considered too dangerous and risky. The next attempt at reform, the Fifth Lateran Council, always had reform at the top of the agenda in the minds of some, and it was frequently invoked by others, but it was never taken in hand with the kind of energy that was required were it to have any practical consequences.

The Fifth Lateran Council and Reform in Its Own Words

After repeated calls for a reforming council, the Fifth Lateran Council was finally convened on 3 May 1512, at the end of the pontificate of Julius II. It lasted until 16 March 1517, halfway through that of Pope Leo X. It gathered amidst serious political strife and military action arising from French claims to lands in Italy. These naturally affected the council, for, in order to safeguard his Italian claims, King Louis XII convened a rival council of prelates, theologians, and other church notables in Pisa and then in Milan. Although the partisans of the pope gathered at the Lateran referred to their rival as a "little council" (*conciliabulum*), its existence unfortunately diverted a lot of energy and concentration of the Lateran Fathers away from the "reform of the Church in head and members" that should have been their principal goal.

This complication did not, however, prevent numerous proposals and speeches in favour of reform from taking place both in the council's preparatory meetings and in its actual sessions. The Spanish bishops, with the backing of their king, began a serious reflection on Church reform. Prior to travelling to Rome, they met in synod at

Burgos in November 1511.[7] Citing the Council of Constance's decree *Frequens*,[8] which stated that a general council of the Church must be convened every five years, they called for a decentralization of power from Rome to the bishops. They also proposed that candidates for ecclesiastical benefices be carefully examined prior to appointment. Archbishop Diego de Deza of Seville, a Dominican friar who was famous for his advocacy for Christopher Columbus, convened a provincial council in 1512 that recommended a long list of juridical measures to be adopted at the Lateran.[9] As a result, King Ferdinand dispatched his prelates and ambassadors to the Lateran Council armed with precise instructions about legal issues. They called for the clarification of the rival ecclesiologies that had arisen between the papacy and the conciliarist doctrines of the fifteenth century.

Two learned and saintly Venetian Camaldolese Hermits, Tommaso (Paolo) Giustiniani and Vincenzo (Pietro) Quirini, addressed a *Libellus*[10] to Pope Leo X that went much further in denouncing abuses in the Church and proposing solutions to end them. The eremetical vocations of these two humanist hermits had come late in life after a pilgrimage to the Holy Land led to a spiritual conversion. Both having served as diplomats in the service of Venice, they were familiar with the world of politics and culture and were able to bring to bear a lucid judgment on the situation of the Church. By looking first at different states of life and then at the different levels of the hierarchy, they arrived at harsh but accurate diagnoses of both the avarice of princes, which posed great danger when they intervened in

7   This preparatory synod at Burgos is not documented in Mansi.
8   See Norman P. Tanner, *Decrees of the Ecumenical Councils* (London; Washington, D.C., 1990), 1: *438–43. This work gives the texts in their original languages with a facing English translation. (= Tanner, *Decrees*.)
9   Mansi 32: 579–650.
10 English translations of salient parts of the *Libellus* can be found in an analysis by Giuseppe Alberigo, "The Reform of the Episcopate in the *Libellus* to Leo X by the Camaldolese Hermits Vincenzo Querini and Tommaso Giustiniani," in *Reforming the Church Before Modernity: Patterns, Problems and Approaches*, ed. Christopher M. Bellitto and Louis I. Hamilton (Aldershot, Hants.; Burlington, Vt., 2005), 139–52. For the Latin text see *Annales Camaldulenses ordinis Sancti Benedicti* ... , ed. J.B. Mittarelli and A. Costadoni (Venice, 1755–1773; repr. Farnborough, Hants., 1970), 9: 612–719.

Church affairs, and the ignorance of the laity. They proposed that, to instruct the laity, it was necessary at the very least to translate into vernacular languages the articles of faith, the Epistles, and the Gospels. They believed that the difficulties that the Latin liturgy posed for ordinary lay persons – an issue that would be strongly raised by Protestants – was a serious problem for their faith. They held that the pope's principal role was to be an example in Christian living for the entire Church. Episcopal promotions, they held, should be made strictly on the basis of merit. They proposed that cardinals, instead of receiving revenue from benefices accruing from ecclesiastical positions that they could not exercise, should receive an annual, renewable pension and should have as their duty the annual visitation of different dioceses of Christendom.

Because they were monks, Giustiniani and Quirini left judgment on their own state of life to others, and many of the bishops were eager to do so because of the exempt status of some religious orders. But they did call for strict observance of the Rule, including enclosure, and adherence to constitutional governing procedures in religious orders, such as general chapters. On the wider scene they regarded failures to convene gatherings such as councils, provincial synods, and diocesan synods as among the principal causes for the continued scourge of abuses in the Church.

The Latin discourses of most of the Fathers of Lateran V, often delivered in high-blown rhetorical style, make it clear that reform was very much on their minds. Nevertheless, most of their interventions failed to provide either useful analyses of the root causes of abuses and other difficulties in the Church or viable solutions for them.

Still, it is often helpful to look at the actual words used by some of the speakers, because they clearly yearned for a lost ideal that could be recaptured if juridical norms were once again observed. This is what we read in the opening discourse of the Council pronounced on 15 May 1512 by Giles of Viterbo (c. 1465–1532), superior general of the Augustinian friars (Martin Luther's own order), a Hebrew scholar and one of the most eminent figures of his time.[11]

---

11 Mansi 32: 669–76. For an English translation see *The Catholic Reformation: Savonarola to Ignatius Loyola; Reform in the Church, 1495–1540*, ed. John C. Olin (New York; Evanston, Ill., 1969; repr. New York, 1992), 41–53. (= Olin.)

Some said that Giles' description of the abuses in the Church brought tears to the eyes of the assembled prelates. He opened with an apocalyptic contrast between the modern Church, now devoid of its pristine lustre, and a Golden Age stretching from the time of Christ to Constantine.[12] This theme of corruption as the product of ecclesiastical wealth is, of course, a celebrated and recurrent one in the history of the Church. Giles traced it back to the official recognition of Christianity, prior to which the Church had been poor and had lived in danger of martyrdom. Giles outlines nine periods in the decline of the Church. In this he is not much different from many other critics, beginning with Joachim of Fiore (1135–1202). Just as Christ, asleep in a boat buffeted by a storm,[13] had to be awakened, so the dormant if not moribund Church must be revived![14] "Restoration," "revival," "recovery": those are the words that Giles of Viterbo uses frequently to describe the tasks of the Council.

Another council Father, the learned Dominican Master General Tommaso de Vio, usually known as Cajetan, was a champion of papal authority. In his 17 May discourse, he railed against the rival, schismatic council gathered at Pisa.[15] He distinguished the Church, which is holy, from its members, lay or clerical, who are all sinners. His ecclesiology depicts Jerusalem, our "mother," as the perfect city where the sacraments, the saints, the apostles and doctors, the gifts of the Holy Spirit, the power of the keys, and the revelation of angels all reside.[16] Analogically, this heavenly Jerusalem is holy as God is holy; but its citizens, the daughter Church here on earth, inevitably fall into error. It is the task of the pope and the council to overcome what is "deformed" and "depraved," aiming at a four-fold goal: reform (*reformatio*) of the Church; restitution (*restitutio*) of morals; rejection (*revocatio*) of heretics; and infusion (*roboratio*) of new life into old laws. Using the same strategies as he did in reforming the Dominicans at this same time, Cajetan proposes a strengthening of the rule of

12   Mansi 32: 670A.
13   Mansi 32: 670B.
14   Mansi 32: 674A.
15   Mansi 32: 719–27.
16   Mansi 32: 720D–21A.

law and a better way of choosing men to carry out that task. Several years later, Cajetan would be delegated by the pope to examine and confront Luther.

Numerous other council Fathers delivered discourses calling for reform of the Church. Almost all of them deployed similar rhetorical approaches. A good example is the young archbishop of Siponto, Giovanni Maria del Monte, who would later be a papal legate to the Council of Trent before becoming Pope Julius III. In a kind of academic exercise he calls for the "restitution" – restitutio again – of justice, drawing this insight from the Divine Institutes of Lactantius, a work in which that early Christian historian incorporates the Hellenic vision of a Golden Age.[17] But one looks in vain in del Monte's discourse for either an analysis of the cause of the Church's troubles or for concrete remedies proposed for them.

Some of the Council members thought the best way to revive the Church would be a renewed crusade against the Turks. This was the opinion of Giovanni-Battista Gargha, a Hospitaller from Siena. In his sermon on 19 December 1513, he tried to convince the delegates that a renewal of Latin Christendom and of the Church would follow such a military victory.[18] Leo X issued a bull on 5 May 1514 urging Christian rulers to make peace among themselves so that an expedition against the enemies of the Christian faith might be realized.[19]

Apart from a proposal like that, most of the conciliar interventions were content with eloquent exhortations to return to the instituta of the Church: its laws, customs and traditions, and the magisterium of the Scriptures, the Fathers and doctors. An example is Bernard Zanni, primate of Dalmatia, who spoke on 10 May 1512.[20] Such reminders of the foundational elements in the life of the Church are not without interest; but they offered no solutions to a crisis that was indeed a profound one.

Although we can conclude that many of the delegates to the Fifth Lateran Council at least tried to identify the pressing difficulties of the

17 Lactantius, Divine Institutes 7.24.1, ed. and trans. Anthony Bowen and Peter Garnsey (Liverpool, 2003), 434–6.
18 Mansi 32: 855.
19 Tanner, Decrees 1: *609–14.
20 Mansi 32: 702.

Church, we must also conclude that they avoided making decisions about the really controversial issues. The council's principal accomplishments were, first, the recognition of the union of Maronite Christians with Rome. Although that union had been negotiated in the thirteenth century, it was only now fully implemented by the Holy See. A second result was that Lateran V ratified the Concordat[21] between King Francis I and Pope Leo X which, following a war that was won by the French, effected a reconciliation between France and the papacy and normalized French-papal relations for centuries to come. It gave immense advantages to the French kings, such as appointment of bishops and abbots, but it also provided a strong incentive to keep the French monarchy allied to the papacy – an important factor indeed for the crucial choices that French kings would make during the sixteenth century.

Certain other contemporary problems received attention and nuanced solutions at the Fifth Lateran Council. For example, the council ratified earlier, implicit approval of *Monti di pietà*,[22] a kind of credit union which loaned money at a low rate of interest. The council also gave a ruling on the "new art" of printing from movable type. It was described as a gift from God but was at the same time seen as a potential source of trouble. The council Fathers therefore took measures to provide means of censuring dangerous books before they could be printed.[23]

We should not conclude that Lateran V never tried to bring about internal reforms in the Church. To the contrary, several conciliar texts attempted to do so, but in the end they amounted to nothing more than pious wishes. The bull *Superne dispositionis arbitrio*,[24] voted by the council on 5 May 1514, was intended to deal with abuses in the benefice system by raising the ages required for nomination to bishoprics (thirty years of age, with possible dispensation for those

---

21 Tanner, *Decrees* 1: *638–9.
22 Offering credit at low interest was now regarded as a pious act, a form of charity, hence the use of *pietà*; *monte*, meaning literally "mountain" or "hill," referred to the "heap" of the capital fund. The bull approving it was *Inter multiplices* (4 May 1515). See Tanner, *Decrees* 1: *625–7.
23 See *Inter sollicitudines* in Tanner, *Decrees* 1: *632–3.
24 Tanner, *Decrees* 1: *614–25; see also Olin, 54–64.

only twenty-seven years old). It also tried to deal with the practice of creating commendatory abbots and priors of monasteries; but the text provided for so many exceptions that it was, in effect, empty of any positive content. Moreover, the will to enforce it was completely lacking, even at the highest level. For example, just three weeks after passage of the bull, Pope Leo X blatantly violated its provisions by giving a canonry to an eight-year-old child. Then, on 26 July 1515, he made a fifteen-year-old Portuguese prince a bishop.

Actually, as early as 1517 a remarkable program for reform was presented to the Council, the *De reformandis moribus* of Giovanni-Francesco Pico della Mirandola (1469–1533). Like his illustrious uncle, the irenic polyglot philosopher Giovanni Pico della Mirandola, Giovanni-Francesco had come under the reforming spell of Savonarola. His proposal therefore insisted on a return to the *instituta*, the old laws – including the precepts of natural law. He especially stressed the power and the necessity of good example, warning that as long as popes, bishops, and princes failed to observe laws and to do what was good, it was hopeless to think that their inferiors, observing them, would ever be able to distinguish good from evil. He conceded that a hierarchical and aristocratic conception like this at least had the advantage of singling out – and placing the blame on – those who should be the agents of reform in Christianity. In clearly denouncing many of the council interventions that were so general as to be empty, Giovanni-Francesco sought to go beyond the indecisiveness of Lateran V. He advocated a moral and intellectual reform.[25]

Just as Savonarola had employed an apocalyptic approach which had seduced his compatriots but then left them feeling abandoned, so did Giovanni-Francesco Pico della Mirandola underplay the reform of Church structures while emphasizing that only a strong commitment of the will could effect a renewal in the Church. As a humanist, he called for a return to *pietas*, to a Christian way of life, and to *paideia*, that best of educating ideals inherited from Antiquity. He thus

25 The discourse (or letter) of Giovanni-Francesco Pico della Mirandola appears neither in Mansi nor in the *Decreta et acta concilii Lateranensis* (Rome, 1521). Early printed texts of it appeared in Haguenau (1520) and Bologna (1523); see Olin, 55 n7.

stressed the formation of the clergy and the need to prepare and distribute the best editions of Sacred Scripture and liturgical texts. This same ideal would also preoccupy many who worked for Catholic reform a half-century later. But Giovanni-Francesco Pico della Mirandola's stirring proposals arrived too late for Lateran V to take into account. We can only speculate whether the council Fathers would have bothered to consider them.

The judgment of historians about the Fifth Lateran Council is a rather severe one. Ignaz von Döllinger (1799–1890), a leader of the anti-Vatican I "Old Catholics," saw it as a mere sketch, a "draft" for the later Council of Trent. As we have seen, Lateran V never actually dealt with the problems confronting the Church. Aside from its condemnation of the doctrine of "double truth" proposed by Pomponazzi (1462–1525) and the Aristotelian school of Padua, the Council paid scant attention to theological or philosophical questions. It had no sense of the storms which were about to break out over Catholic doctrine. As well, it showed scant awareness of the important fact that nothing could be changed in the Church without a moral and spiritual reform. In these ways Lateran V resembled the condemnation, fifteen years earlier, of Savonarola. There is little to be seen in its eloquent speeches and carefully drafted documents of the need for the kind of interior religion that the *devotio moderna* had espoused and that Christian humanists like Erasmus were proposing. To borrow the expression of one of the best authorities on Lateran V, its attempt at reform was locked out by the entrenched system that was already in place.[26] This is certainly what Martin Luther sensed when he commented on the Council shortly after it closed: "The *reformatio* needed in the Church will require more than a pontiff and a lot of cardinals. It will require the efforts of the entire world or, rather, of God alone [*sed totius orbis, immo solius Dei*]. Only the One who has brought us to

---

26   Nelson H. Minnich, *The Fifth Lateran Council (1512–17)* (Aldershot, Hants., 1993). See also his "The Last Two Councils of the Catholic Reformation: The Influence of Lateran V on Trent," in *Early Modern Catholicism: Essays in Honour of John W. O'Malley, S.J.*, ed. Kathleen M. Comerford and Hilmar M. Pabel (Toronto, 2001), 3–25.

these times knows the right time for this reformation."[27] Luther wrote these lines shortly after he went public with his *Ninety-five Theses*, thus adding another dimension to the already enormous task waiting to be accomplished. Still, the professor from Wittenberg was probably not yet aware that, just a few months later, he would consider himself to be the instrument chosen by God to reform the Church and that he was duty-bound to answer that call.

27 Martin Luther, *Resolutiones disputationum de indulgentiarum virtute*, in *D. Martin Luthers Werke: Kritische Gesamtausgabe. Weimarer Ausgabe* (Weimar, 1883–), 1: 627, lines 27–9. (= WA.)

     Not in *Luther's Works,* ed. Jaroslav Pelikan et al. (St Louis, Mo., 1955–1986). (= *LW.*)

CHAPTER THREE

Claims of Reform

All the Churches that were born in the sixteenth century, whether they were called – or called themselves – "Protestant," "Reformed," or "Evangelical," can be grouped together historically into the broad movement of that time that favoured a renewal of Latin Christendom independent of the papacy. As time went on, the men who founded those Churches or provided inspiration for their establishment would claim that they had made possible a viable form and structure for this long hoped for, but never before realized, aspiration.

Once this has been recognized, the historian must look very closely at what those founders – Luther, Zwingli, Butzer, Calvin, and many others – said or wrote about what they hoped to do and what they thought they had accomplished. He must then try to find the answers to several questions, such as: Did they consider themselves to be Reformers? Were they aware of having reformed the Church? How had they planned to go about doing this? How did they justify doing what they did without receiving the stamp of approval of the traditional Church? When and why did they arrive at the point of constituting autonomous ecclesial communities? Posing questions of this sort raises enormous implications for ecumenism. Suggesting answers for them raises the stakes yet higher – even though the four centuries of existing separated from the Roman Church and from each other weigh more heavily on ecumenism than any insights we might discover about the original intentions of their founders.

Martin Luther, Instrument of the Word

We have already noted how Luther longed to see a truly renewed Church and how he understood that it could only be accomplished by God alone. The failure of the papacy and of the councils as God's instruments of reform became so evident to him in the years 1518–1520 that he dismissed the infallibility and even the viability of both. In his opinion, the reform of the Church would have to be accomplished by other means.

The road to reform therefore had to be more than a simple wish to correct abuses or to plan structural modifications. Nor could it be simply a moral or spiritual reform, as Savonarola – whom Luther looked upon as a precursor – had seen it. He concluded that reform must be based on a new approach to theology. It must reject the centuries of tradition and of interpretation of the Word of God that had led the Church down the wrong path.

This was indeed what the historian Lucien Febvre, whom we cited in the first chapter, concluded in his analysis of the Lutheran Reformation and also of the Reformation movement in France. True, the Protestant Reformers ardently denounced abuses in the Catholic Church; but their plans were primarily aimed at a thorough change in Church doctrine. According to Febvre's celebrated expression, they did not reproach the Roman Church so much for living badly as for believing wrongly – or, more exactly, the Reformers believed the Church lived badly because it believed wrongly.

A line from Luther's celebrated *Table Talk* says it clearly: "The papists want to reform the Church by changing external ceremonies and amending morals; but if the doctrine is not reformed the reform of morals is in vain, because the idolatry of false sanctity can only be recognized by the Word and faith."[1]

As early as 1512, Luther declared that "the pivot, the essential element of a legitimate reformation and the kernel of all piety" is to abandon all the human doctrines and the fables that had developed, and then to discern the meaning of the pure Gospel and to announce the word of truth with fear and respect.[2]

In 1518 Luther affirmed in more specific terms his criteria for a radical purification of Catholic doctrine: "I simply believe that it is impossible to reform the Church unless the canons, the decretals, scholastic theology, philosophy, and logic that are presently taught and held are destroyed and that different forms of learning be put in their place. In this opinion I continue to pray daily to the Lord, until he comes again, that the pure study of the Bible and of the Holy Fathers be reestablished."[3]

1 WA *Tischreden* 4: 232, no. 1539. Not in *LW*.
2 *Sermo praescriptus praeposito in Litzka* (1512), WA 1: 13. Not in *LW*.
3 Letter to Jodocus Trutfetter (9 May 1518), WA *Briefwechsel* 1: 170, no. 74, lines 33–6. Not in *LW*.

This was not the wish of a humanist intellectual who, believing in the importance of the Bible and the Fathers, calls for a return to the sources. It was a much more radical demand to liberate the Word of God which, according to Luther, was being held in shackles by the Roman Church. The vocabulary of imprisonment and servitude is one that the Wittenberg reformer used frequently. One of his major works of 1520 which would precipitate the rupture with Rome was blatantly entitled *The Babylonian Captivity of the Church*. Its theme was that, just as the people of Israel had been deported as prisoners behind the walls of Babylon, so is the Church imprisoned by three walls, one of which was the papacy's monopoly on the interpretation of Sacred Scripture. Luther would frequently present his approach to reformation in terms of liberation, especially the destruction of the bastion of Rome.

The occasion which Luther chose to make his initial declaration, the *Ninety-five Theses* that he made public on 31 October 1517, is symbolic of his journey. In the beginning, he challenged what could seem to be a simple abuse: he denounced the excessive and abusive preaching of indulgences – doubly so in the case of Johann Tetzel, whose doubtful theology, geared to fleece simple people, the Church itself had condemned. But from simply denouncing abuses in 1517 Luther's *Babylonian Captivity* passed to what he considered the source of all abuses in the Church: a doctrinal deviation touching the power of the keys, the sacrament of Penance, and even the communion of saints. The importance of the *Ninety-five Theses* remains in that, although he began by merely denouncing a scandalous and local practice, he ended up by implicitly calling into question the whole theological system and devotional practice of the Church. Vigilant Catholic theologians, his first critics, understood this right away. Even Erasmus, who was an unsparing critic of the excessive practice of pilgrimages, never touched the edifice of the Church itself. Luther, even in attacking indulgences, did not pull back from his efforts to lay it waste.

Did Luther see himself as the one whom God had chosen to renew the Church? The answer must be "yes." Was it something in which he took pride? The answer must be "no" – at least in the usual meaning of the word "pride." Luther certainly never referred to himself as the Reformer of the Church, but he was very much aware of the radical, resounding impact of his writings and of his own genius. In a foundational text dating from 1528, ten years after the *Ninety-five Theses*, he was already able to draw up a positive summation of his "Reformation" vis-à-vis the whole Catholic Church. Some things, he wrote, had to be set aside, while others needed to be brought to the forefront:

> I think that I have achieved a Reformation ... .
>
> First of all, in the realm of books I pushed the papists toward Sacred Scripture and chased away the pagan Aristotle and the theologians with their Summas and Books of *Sentences*, so much so that they no longer hold sway in pulpits and teach in schools in the manner they used to do ... .
>
> I have also weakened their taste for pomp and the seductive trafficking in indulgences ... .
>
> Thirdly I have almost succeeded in shutting down pilgrimages; and I have accomplished many other things that the papists ought to have done themselves ... .
>
> Moreover, with God's help I have been the cause of this: that our little seven-year-old boys and girls know more about Christian doctrine than the doctors in universities ever knew in past times. The true catechism is once again taught in our little group. By this I mean the Our Father, the true faith, the ten commandments, the real meaning of Penance, Baptism, prayer, the cross, life, death, the sacrament of the altar, as well as what marriage, temporal authority, father and mother, woman and child, servant and maid-servant really mean ... . This is the reformation of Luther.[4]

This text reveals quite a bit about Luther's position. First of all, speaking in the first person, he attributes to himself this revolution in doctrine and comportment. His conclusions, although premature, in their totality show quite well the scope of what had been changed and what still remained to be changed: the new stress on Sacred Scripture; the abandoning of scholasticism that was in servitude to pagan

4 Preface to the *Von Priester Ehe des wirdigen Licentiam Steffan Klingebeyl* (1528), WA 26: 530, lines 7–35. Not in *LW*.

philosophy; the true doctrine of the sacraments; the meaning of Christianity, of the family, and of the condition of the baptized Christian. What was left of the old edifice? In a reflection written in 1541, Luther's satisfaction is evident: "Yes, we have a beautiful, pure, and holy Church – one such as existed in the time of the apostles."[5]

Luther's euphoria and pride in having faced up to his adversaries is evident. We see this again in an earlier declaration that he made in 1534: "The papists do not want to be reformed, as they say, by a friar like me. But even so, that friar (and here I must brag a little – but secretly, so that they do not learn of it) has indeed reformed them quite a lot. Thanks be to God, with my Gospel I have reformed them more than they could ever do with five councils."[6] It should be noted that Luther seems to take credit here for stimulating, if not some actual reforms on the Catholic side, at least a heightening awareness among Catholics of the need for reform.

Still, Luther never explicitly gives himself the title of "Reformer" or of "prophet." This was not only because, as a German and a humanist, he preferred to present himself as a "doctor" in theology or Sacred Scripture but also because he saw himself as "caught up in the stream of events" in which God acted through him. Innumerable texts of Luther show that, in very Pauline terms, he assimilates his doctrine with the Gospel or simply with the truth. As Marc Lienhard has said, Luther presents himself as an evangelist, a preacher, a simple servant of God, and a witness to Jesus Christ, "all of whom Christ esteems as far superior to doctors and councils."[7]

Luther was obviously too intelligent not to have asked himself, "The theologians and the saints who came before you, or the Church before you came along, were they all totally in error? Are you the only one who has been guided by the Holy Spirit?"[8] As well, he was too tormented not to have pondered with anguish the damage, scandals,

---

5   *Wider Hans Worst*, WA 51: 536. See *Against Hanswurst*, in *LW* 41: 185–256.

6   *Ein Brief ... von seinem Buch der Winkelmessen* (1534), WA 38: 270, lines 1–4. Not in *LW*.

7   *Von den neuen Eckischen Bullen und Lügen* (1520), WA 6: 581, lines 10–15. Not in *LW*.

8   *Tröstung an die Ehristen zu Halle* (1527), WA 23: 421, lines 27–8. Not in *LW*.

and divisions that his preaching engendered.[9] But, even though he was haunted by his mission, in a certain sense he depended on these very contradictions, these trials, in order to draw from them a redoubled energy and a confirmation of the choices he made.

Yet Luther never consented, at least in theory, to give his name to a Church. He invoked Corinthians 3:4 in this regard: "I insist that no one ever use my name and call himself Lutheran rather than Christian. How could I, a poor vessel of stinking flesh destined for worms, ever allow that my miserable name be given to children of Christ?"[10] This text certainly proves that Luther did not want to found a new Church – not even a reformed one – but rather that he intended to gather the whole Church into the return to true religion as he expounded it. For him it was the traditional Church which had become a sect: "It is the papists who ought to be called sectarians because, not satisfied with teaching in the name of Christ, they also want to be disciples of the pope."[11] In other words, describing himself as an unworthy instrument of God, Luther set in motion this return to true doctrine, and that constituted the only reform worthy of the name. In rejecting Luther's teaching, he was convinced, the followers of the pope had excluded themselves from that one true reform.

The "extraordinary ministry" of Calvin[12]

Unlike Luther, Butzer, and Zwingli, John Calvin was never ordained in the Roman Church. Coming on the scene a generation after Luther, however, he likewise claimed for himself a role in the reform of the Church. Alexandre Ganoczy[13] has written about Calvin's

9   *De servo arbitrio*, WA 18: 625, lines 13–16. English trans. by Philip S. Watson and Benjamin Drewery, *Bondage of the Will*, in *LW* 33.
10 *Eine treue Bermahnung zu allen Christen* (1522), WA 8: 684, lines 4–11. Not in *LW*.
11 Ibid., lines 11–12.
12 A number of biographies and studies of Calvin exist, and many more are appearing in anticipation of the 500th anniversary of his birth (1509). A recent and very readable study in English is that of Randall C. Zachman, *John Calvin as Teacher, Pastor, and Theologian: The Shape of His Writings and Thought* (Grand Rapids, Mich., 2006).
13 Ganoczy, *Le jeune Calvin: Genèse et évolution de sa vocation réformatrice* (Wiesbaden, 1966).

"reformist vocation." Even apart from the important doctrinal differences that existed between them, Calvin described his vocation as a reformer in ways quite different from that of Luther.

In his *Institutes of the Christian Religion*, which the young Calvin wrote in Basel in 1536 and which he constantly reworked and enlarged, he affirmed both his doctrine and his own conversion. Three years later, in his letter to Cardinal Jacopo Sadoleto,[14] he explained why Geneva was not prepared to return to communion with the Church of Rome. In the same way, in the *Institutes* he develops fully and in depth a double theme – one positive and one negative – showing how he viewed his reformer's task to be accomplished. Here again, as with Luther, Calvin saw his task as one concerned not with practical matters but with theological ones.

Calvin's notion of reformation meant returning to "true religion," to "true piety," because both were still entombed in the Roman Church. Actually, Calvin hardly ever employs the word *reformatio* or the verb "to reform." Instead he usually describes the Church in other terms: it is "deformed" or "disfigured." What must be rediscovered is the true "piety" that is found in the Gospel. The word *pietas* was very popular in the fifteenth and sixteenth centuries and especially in the ranks of humanists. Calvin used it to denote the right attitude of the believer, a religious way of living, of adhering to true doctrine. *Pietas* was thus a composite of virtuous comportment and good theology. For Calvin it combined what at that time was usually meant by "religion" and what, in modern and Catholic language, would be called "sanctity."

The Christian piety of which Calvin wrote was to be the product of instruction, of formation – what the French language of that time called *institution*. Through reading, preaching, and meditating the Scriptures one discovers the plan of God who, moved by a paternal piety,[15] sent his Son to save mankind from sin. In return, men and women must relate to God by a true, filial piety.[16] This piety is

14 See *A Reformation Debate: Sadoleto's Letter to the Genevans and Calvin's Reply*, ed. John C. Olin (New York, 1966; repr. 2000).

15 John Calvin, *Opera selecta*, ed. Petrus Barth, Dora Scheuner, and Wilhelm Niesel (Munich, 1926–1963), 1: 106, 221.

16 Calvin, *Opera selecta* 1: 59, 76.

Christocentric, because it is only through the incarnate Son that the Christian is able to turn his thoughts to God. For Calvin, that action of turning the thoughts to God etymologically signifies the word "religion." To be pious is to centre oneself on God, his absolute sovereignty, his ineffable and inscrutable will, and to render to him "worship in spirit and in truth." That, Calvin said, has not been possible in the Roman Church for a long time, because the pure Word of God was no longer preached and because worship – the administration of the sacraments – was no longer "rightly" performed. In effect, the preaching of the papists, instead of being centred on what was essential, dealt with what was false and illusory, with magic and superstition. It was rife with Judaism and paganism. This is why Calvin said that the Roman Church had buried the Gospel. This is a frequent theme with him, although he uses the image of a grave illness rather than of the finality of death. Christ's Church in Rome, he says, is still alive, but it is sick and disfigured. It is in fact half-buried (*semisepulta*),[17] a condition which thus renders Christ himself half-buried.[18] The Church is thus, as it were, buried alive[19] and "all but destroyed." An allegory of the same kind has him speaking of "vestiges," of "remnants," by which he means that the only valid and "incorruptible" action remaining in the Roman Church is that of baptizing in the name of the Trinity.[20] Neither Calvin nor Luther ever considered re-baptizing anyone who came to them from the traditional Church. To re-build, to correct, and to re-form the Church, it must possess at least some authentic form as a starting point.

Thus, Calvin looked on the reform of the Church less as the destruction of a fortress, as Luther did, and more as a healing, an "exhumation," and a purification or "return" (*revocatio*) to the model of the primitive Church. What Calvin and his followers said about renewal by means of the Word applies to the whole Church. He emphasizes this in his dedicatory epistle addressed to King Francis I that he placed at the head of the *Institutes*. Calvin did not expect the

17 Calvin, *Opera selecta* 1: 476.
18 Calvin, *Opera selecta* 5: 42.
19 Calvin, *Opera selecta* 1: 22, 25.
20 Calvin, *Opera selecta* 1: 134.

Most Christian King to cooperate in his project of reforming the Church in France. But he wanted at least to persuade him not to deny his Protestant subjects, who were loyal to the king's temporal power, the free practice of their worship.

We should note that Calvin uses neither "Protestant" nor "Catholic" in the confessional sense of those terms. For Roman Catholics he prefers expressions like "those of the pope's kingdom." He resorts to his severest language of "faction" to describe those who pretend to represent the one, whole Church which he regards as invisible.

Calvin believed that, because neither the pope nor a council could ever bring about the healing of the Church that was required, God had seen fit to raise up prophets in the sixteenth century,[21] and Calvin certainly saw himself as one of them. In order to identify his reform movement with the model of the idealized, primitive Church, he borrowed the inspired division of ministries that Martin Butzer, one of the Strasbourg Reformers, had drawn from the New Testament. His followers would have pastors, doctors, elders, and deacons. But he carries it even further when he uses Ephesians 4:11 to distinguish these ordinary ministries from the higher ministries of apostles, prophets, and evangelists. Just as God brought forth these extraordinary ministries in both Testaments of Scripture when the necessity of the times called for them, so has He brought them forth in the present day.[22] When looking back on his own conversion and "extraordinary" vocation, Calvin does not look to the Old Testament prophets. Instead, he recalls the image of Paul on the road to Damascus, and uses the same terminology. Who more than Saint Paul sensed that he was the instrument of the divine will to build up the Church? Thus, even if Calvin rarely uses the term "reform," the exceptional latitude he gives to his own ministry in the Church leaves little room for doubt that he saw himself as one chosen by God to reform the Church.

Up to now we have looked only at the two founding Reformers of the two major Protestant traditions. To do the same for others who also called for a "new faith" would require a different and much longer book than the one we intend. Each one of the Reformers

21 Calvin, *Opera selecta* 1: 234, 245.
22 Calvin, *Opera selecta* 5: 22, 45; 6: 521.

offered different diagnoses of and remedies for the sickness he saw in the traditional Church. Ulrich Zwingli, the Reformer of Zurich, often resorted to this kind of medical vocabulary. In his treatise *On False and True Religion* he concludes that the Church of his time is sick from the *pontificum morbus*, the pontifical malady; and he adds, "Too mild a dose of medicine only prolongs the onset of death. Strong remedies are needed to restore life and health."[23] But even he, a more radical Reformer than Luther or Calvin, wanted to retain – not destroy – the institution of the Church, although he would give it another form – almost another definition. That was true of most of the other "magisterial" Reformations (i.e. those adopted by some "magistracy" or civil authority). Apart from the Anabaptists, no other reform movement in the sixteenth century refused the legitimacy of Baptisms performed in the Roman Church. For Anabaptists, infant baptism is "the greatest and first abomination of the pope."[24] Theirs was no longer a reform in the usual sense of the term. It was the establishment of a sect that all other Protestant theologians saw as a danger to their own ecclesiology.

Catholic authorities and theologians naturally denied that the Protestants had "reformed" the Church. They saw what Luther had done as an "innovation," a different and "new" faith, and described Calvin's work as a "Pretended Reform." Here again we can see in their different viewpoints the conclusion of Lucien Febvre when he wrote:

> It was not the purpose or the desire of men to separate from the Church; quite the contrary, the men in question claimed in all sincerity to be motivated simply by the desire to "restore" it on the pattern of a primitive Church which, acting as a kind of myth, had captured their imagination. "Restoration," "primitive Church" – these were comfortable expressions with which to cover up in their own eyes the very temerity of their secret desires. What they really wanted was not restoration but a com-

---

23 Zwingli, *Huldreich Zwinglis Werke* [and] *Huldrici Zwinglii Opera* (Zurich, 1828–1842), 3: 227.
24 Schleitheim Articles (1527), art. 1, trans. John Howard Yodler. For this document see Karl Koop, ed., *Confessions of Faith in the Anabaptist Tradition, 1527–1660* (Kitchener, Ont.; Scottdale, Pa., 2006), 27.

plete renewal. The ultimate achievement of the Reformation was that it gave the men of the sixteenth century what they were looking for — some confusedly, others entirely lucidly — a religion more suited to their new needs, more in agreement with the changed conditions of their social life — that is what the Reformation finally accomplished.[25]

But, no matter how the different sides viewed it, the Reformation that Luther, Calvin, and other Protestants claimed to have achieved barely touched upon the abuses which had caused the crisis and which sorely needed to be addressed. Claims of reform were revealing that a much more serious crisis was at stake: a profound confrontation about Christian theology.

25 Febvre, "The Origins of the French Reformation: A Badly-put Question?" trans. K. Folka, in *A New Kind of History, from the Writings of Lucien Febvre*, ed. Peter Burke (New York; Evanston, Ill., 1973), 59–60.

CHAPTER FOUR

Preparations for Reform

After studying Luther's books and reviewing his debates with Johann Eck and Cajetan, Rome excommunicated Luther in the bull *Exsurge Domine* on 15 June 1520. Almost a year later, the imperial Diet meeting in Worms on 26 May 1521 placed him under the ban of the Empire. Neither the papal condemnation nor the imperial ban was able to silence Luther, because the Elector of Saxony granted him sanctuary. Even while he was in seclusion, many theologians and pastors across Germany rallied to his call for reform in the Church. Faced with a strong movement that was growing ever more radical, the Roman Church needed to do more than issue condemnations and toothless proposals for reform as it had done at the Fifth Lateran Council.

Suddenly, however, hopes for a real change seemed to be justified when, following the death of Pope Leo X, Adriaan Floriszoon of Utrecht was elected as supreme pontiff in 1522 and assumed the name Adrian VI. A humanist and even an Erasmian, Adrian had been formed initially by the Brethren of the Common Life in his native Holland. He had no connections in Italy, but he had been the tutor of the young German Emperor, Charles V. At his installation on 29 August 1522, Adrian VI seemed to have a firm intention of steering the Church firmly on a path of reform.

Tragically, Adrian died just one year later, on 14 September 1523. We can therefore judge what he might have accomplished only by studying what we can discover about his intentions. These were clearly laid out in a speech that his legate, Francesco Chieregati, delivered in his name at the Diet of Nuremberg on 3 January 1523.[1] In it Adrian urged the Diet to enforce the sanctions imposed against Luther. But he also acknowledged that the sins of priests and prelates had sorely tried the patience of God, and that the sins of the people were only the logical consequence of following the example of their

---

1   For an English translation of Adrian VI's instructions to Chieregati, see Olin, 118–27.

pastors. Citing Saint John Chrysostom, he compared Jesus casting out the moneychangers from the temple to a good doctor attacking an illness at its cause. Just as Jesus denounced the sins of the priests who had allowed profanation of the temple, so the Apostolic See could not be spared condemnation for its many years of giving bad example to the people:

> No wonder that the illness has spread from the head to the members, from the Supreme Pontiffs to the prelates below them. All of us (that is, prelates and clergy), each one of us, have strayed from our paths; not for a long time has anyone done good; no, not even one [Ps. 13 (14):3]. ... [T]herefore, you will promise that we will expend every effort to reform first this Curia, whence perhaps all this evil has come [*unde forte omne hoc malum processit*] so that, as corruption spread from that place to every lower place, the good health and reformation of all may also issue forth [*reformetur*]. We consider ourselves all the more bound to attend to this, the more we perceive the entire world longing for such a reformation [*reformatio*].[2]

Adrian VI also confided to the Diet that he had not aspired to the papacy and would have declined it "except that the fear of God, the uncorrupt manner of our election, and the dread of impending schism because of our refusal forced us to accept it."[3] He hoped to encourage other learned men and virtuous men whose efforts at reform had up to then found no response to join him in this cause. He acknowledges, however, that this would take time, because the evils that beset the Church were many and varied. It was therefore necessary to address first the most serious and most painful of the evils. On the basis of this speech, which was both clear and specific in its denunciations, we can conclude that Adrian VI intended to be a reforming pope. It was evidently not universally acclaimed in Rome.

2   *Deutsche Reichstagsakten unter Kaiser Karl V*, ed. Adolf Wrede (1901; repr. Göttingen, 1965), 3: 397, lines 15–21, 24–5, 27–8; for the complete English translation see Olin, 122–7.

3   Olin, 125.

Adrian VI, the would-be reformer, was replaced by Clement VII (Giulio de' Medici).[4] The new pope was not blind to the need for reform. Encouraged by Gian Matteo Giberti, he took preliminary steps in that direction.[5] But his pontificate was marked by violent events such as the Peasants' War in Germany which, with Luther's approval, was severely repressed. More serious for Clement himself was the devastating Sack of Rome (6 May 1527) by the imperial army, some regiments of which were composed of Luther's supporters. They left a trail of carnage and sacrilege, and Clement barely escaped from falling into their hands. Imperial propaganda and common sentiment saw in this a divine punishment for the sins of Rome. Clement's political alliances were torn apart, and he was soon confronted with King Henry VIII's demand for an annulment of his marriage to Catherine of Aragon, and then with Henry's secession from the Church of Rome.

Clement VII died on 25 September 1534. His successor, Paul III (Alessandro Farnese), was elected on 13 October. Like Clement, he was an Italian Renaissance prelate who practiced nepotism with abandon. Paradoxically, however, he was to be the pope who would finally open the Roman Church to the possibility of a real reform. This was partly due to the increasingly radical changes in the European religious situation. Probably the most important of these was the Diet of Augsburg (1530), which was incontestably a watershed in the religious history of the sixteenth century. At that Diet the various Protestant reform movements – the name "Protestant" dates only from the preceding year – came to the conclusion that they needed a more structured organization. Expositions of their faith were prepared and were presented to the emperor by the different movements. They evolved into confessional creeds. The most celebrated one, laying out Lutheran doctrine and prepared for the Diet itself,

4 An illegitimate son of Giuliano de' Medici, who had been assassinated in Florence, he was raised by his uncle Lorenzo de' Medici who educated him with his own sons, one of whom became Pope Leo X (1513–1521).

5 Ludwig von Pastor, *The History of the Popes: from the Close of the Middle Ages, Drawn from the Secret Archives of the Vatican and other Original Sources*, ed. and trans. F.I. Antrobus et al. (London; St Louis, Mo., 1891–1961), 10: 378–81.

took the name of "Confession of Augsburg."[6] The era of rival and separate confessional Churches had arrived.

Although Paul III created two commissions to investigate particular abuses, the first years of his pontificate gave little cause to hope that he would be a serious advocate of church reform. For example, he paid political debts by naming cardinals, and he raised members of his own family to the College of Cardinals as well. However, he did choose some cardinals of great ability and value who were aware of the depths of the crisis and were committed to finding a resolution to it.

A bull, promulgated on 23 August 1535, mentioned a future council and proposed to reform the city of Rome and the Roman Curia. It was issued in a traditional format and appeared to apply only to the pope's own diocese – similar, in a way, to what Pope John XXIII did in 1960 – but in this case there was no follow-through, and it came to nothing. But Paul III's determination became more clear in 1536 when he called for a council to meet in Mantua. Although that council never met, the bull set up a committee of eight persons to study the issue of reform. None of them belonged to the inner circle of the Roman Curia. They were Gasparo Contarini,[7] a lay Venetian diplomat who was created a cardinal on 21 May 1535; Gian Pietro Carafa, the co-founder of the Theatine Order and later Pope Paul IV; Reginald Pole, cousin of and, from this time on, adversary of England's King Henry VIII; Jacopo Sadoleto, humanist bishop of Carpentras; Gian Matteo Giberti, reforming bishop of Verona; Federico Fregoso, archbishop of Salerno; two members of religious orders: the Dominican friar Tommaso Badia, Master of the Sacred Palace, and Gregorio Cortese, the Benedictine abbot of San Giorgio Maggiore in the Laguna of Venice; and, finally, Girolamo Aleandro, a diplomat who had extensive knowledge of the situation in Germany.

6   See above, p. 10.
7   Twenty years earlier, in 1516, Contarini had written a treatise on the office of bishop that shows his intelligent concern for reform in the Church. As it was written prior to any public statement of Luther about reform in the Church, it is another strong argument against the notion that reform in the Roman Church was merely a reaction to Protestantism. For an English translation of this treatise see Olin, 90–106.

Would this committee be just one more in a long list of committees whose work would lead to nothing? Sadoleto was not very optimistic. Replying to a letter from Contarini early in 1536, he wrote, "The whole body of Christendom is sick; it suffers from an illness which is beyond relief at this time." He added that it would take a good deal of time and quiet perseverance "to restore health and dignity to the Church."[8] Despite such pessimism, the eight members began their work in secret in November 1536. A month later, Paul III showed his confidence in them when he elevated Carafa, Pole, and Sadoleto to the College of Cardinals. Working rapidly, the committee finished its work and submitted its formal report to the pope on 9 March 1537. It was entitled *Consilium de emendanda ecclesia* (*Counsel concerning the Church which Must be Reformed*).[9]

The Committee delegated Contarini to read the report to twelve other cardinals, all of whom had been members of past reform committees, who were gathered in the Vatican's Camera di Papagallo. Sadoleto then read a separate report about the committee's work. The assembly had no immediate reaction, but its silence would not last long.

The opening lines of the *Consilium* congratulate Paul III for his desire and initiatives taken to reform the Church. The Holy Spirit, it states, "has decided to rebuild through you the Church of Christ, tottering, nay, in fact collapsed, and, as we see, to apply your hand to this ruin."[10] The report then proceeds to carry out the committee's mandate to make known to him the abuses which, by a slow, indiscernible process, had brought such complete ruin to the Church.

The *Consilium* moves immediately to expose with fearless honesty the root of these troubles:

---

8   Sadoleto, *Opera quae exstant omnia: Quorum plura sparsim vagabantur, quaedam doctorum virorum cura nunc primum prodeunt* (Verona, 1737–1738; repr. Ridgewood, N.J., 1964) 1: 216.

9   *Concilium Tridentinum: diariorum, actorum, epistularum tractatuum nova collectio*, ed. Societas Goerresiana (Freiburg-im-Breisgau, 1963–1967), 12: 131–45. (= *CT*.)

    For the English translation of the *Consilium de emendanda ecclesia*, see Olin, 182–97.

10 *Consilium*, in Olin, 186.

Some popes, your predecessors, in the words of the Apostle Paul, "having itching ears, heaped up to themselves teachers according to their own lusts" [2 Tim. 4:3] ... who taught that the pope is the lord of all benefices and that therefore, since a lord may sell by right what is his own, it necessarily follows that the pope cannot be guilty of simony. Thus the will of the pope ... is the [sole] rule governing his activities and deeds: whence it may be shown without doubt that whatever pleases him is also permitted. From this source, as from a Trojan horse, so many abuses and such grave diseases have rushed in upon the Church of God that we now see her afflicted almost to the despair of salvation ... .[11]

But because Paul III [the *Consilium* continues], following the Gospel, knows that he is not a master but a good servant, it can be said to him: "you have resolved to turn from what is unlawful, nor do you wish to be able to do what you should not ... ."[12] The committee is thus convinced of the absolute necessity that every pope observe Church laws without resorting to dispensations except for grave and necessary reasons. Driving the point home, the text states explicitly: "It cannot be permitted even to the Vicar of Christ to obtain any profit in the use of the power of the keys conferred on him by Christ. For truly this is the command of Christ: 'Freely you have received, freely give' [Matt. 10:8]."[13]

From its very beginning, then, the *Consilium* goes to the heart of the crisis by questioning practices permitted by the prevailing church practice and by proposing a moral diagnosis of its faults. By posing the question, "What are the limits of papal power?" it challenges many of the prerogatives, the practices, and the doctrines of the time. This, obviously, would be the most contested part of the report, as far as the Roman Curia was concerned. It should be noted, however – and we can see it in other works of Contarini – that the *Consilium* never calls into question the divine institution of the papacy. Rather, by holding that papal government must, first of all, observe the great precept of divine law, the precept of charity, it challenges the

11 *Consilium*, in Olin, 186–7.
12 *Consilium*, in Olin, 187.
13 Ibid.

presuppositions that come with an exaggerated idea of the papacy. Popes must adhere to positive law and tradition and to natural law, which includes the liberty of man. Actually, the *Consilium* does little more than call into question everything a pope might do that is merely arbitrary and outside the laws of God and man.

But the eight astute prelates do delve very much into particular problems, some of them quite technical. We need be concerned here only with the document's principal criticisms of ecclesiastical affairs and with the remedies, most of them quite precise, that it proposes. One-by-one it evokes issues such as the deplorable state of clerical recruitment, the ordination of candidates who are badly or not at all prepared and of candidates of immoral character. It inveighs against "diabolical" juridical manipulation and the system of awarding benefices. "A benefice in Spain or in Britain then must not be conferred on an Italian, or vice versa."[14] It calls for the end of non-residence at all levels of the hierarchy, an evil which necessarily follows the accumulation of benefices by any one person. The Committee believes that the cardinals, who have oversight of the government of the universal Church, should not be appointed as ordinaries of a diocese – and certainly not of more than one! The text denounces "the great crime, the most pernicious of all," the purchase of dispensation from an illegality, a hypocritical practice that re-doubles the seriousness of the sin.

The *Consilium* then turns its attention to the ways of life of the Christian people and of non-exempt religious orders, to the practice of collecting money for indulgences, and to the absence of any control over what is being taught and what is being printed. Curiously the only name mentioned in this last regard is that of Erasmus, whose best-selling *Colloquies* are said to be dangerous for boys in grammar school. This was perhaps a concession by the humanist members of the committee to those members who were more conservative.

Finally, the *Consilium* lists abuses requiring reform in the city of Rome itself, and here the authors pull no punches. They complain of "priests, some of whom are vile, ignorant, and who celebrate Mass in Saint Peter's while clothed in robes and vestments which they

14 *Consilium*, in Olin, 189.

cannot decently wear in our churches"; of courtesans parading with clerics in broad daylight; and of endemic feuds and violence among private citizens.[15]

The conclusion of the *Consilium* seems to say: There! Now our consciences are clear. But the eight authors were fully aware of the limitations that prudence had forced them to impose in their report. They express hopes mixed with a certain fear: "we hope that you have been chosen to restore in our hearts and in our works the name of Christ now forgotten ... to heal the ills, to lead back the sheep of Christ into one fold, to turn away from us the wrath of God and that vengeance which we deserve, already prepared and looming over our heads."[16]

The reactions expressed in Rome were on the whole quite far from what the eight had hoped. Many Romans naturally feared that such a self-evaluation by the Church would only reinforce the arguments and increase the mockery of the Protestants. They tried to impose secrecy about the proceedings, and they decreed a prohibition against the publication of the *Consilium*, but the former leaked out, and unauthorized printed copies enjoyed a wide diffusion. Johann Sturm, the celebrated Strasbourg schoolmaster, rejoiced to see such a lucid presentation come out of Rome, but he lamented that it had come too late and regretted that it omitted dealing directly with preaching the Gospel. Martin Luther had nothing favourable to say about it and even lampooned it when he commented on its translation into German.[17]

In a Roman consistory the Dominican Cardinal Nikolaus von Schönberg expressed the reservations of many conservatives about the *Consilium*.[18] He was joined by Bartolomeo Guidiccione, a close

15 *Consilium*, in Olin, 196.
16 *Consilium*, in Olin, 197.
17 *Ratschlag eines Ausschusses etlicher Kardinale, Papst Paulo III* (1538), WA 50: 283–308; English trans. by Lewis W. Spitz, in *LW* 34: 235–67.
18 This was reported by Paolo Sarpi, *Istoria del Concilio Tridentino* (London, 1619). Three modern Italian editions exist: Bari, 1935; Florence, 1966; Turin, 1974. Sarpi's anti-Roman bias is manifest in the title of the 1620 English translation: *The Historie of the Councel of Trent: In which are declared ... the practises of the court of Rome, to hinder the Reformation of their errors, and to maintaine their greatnesse.* Selections from Sarpi's *History of the Council of Trent* also appear with his *History of Benefices*, ed. Peter Burke (New York, 1967).

confidant of Pope Paul III. How could the Church's own government, they asked, pass such a radical judgment on its administration of matters which, both juridically and financially, had been part of the institution for two centuries? And could one give the impression of questioning any of the juridical bases for the papacy's claim to plenitude of power?

Paul III nevertheless resolved to examine how he might restructure the pontifical Datary, the curial organization charged with investigating and granting (or refusing to grant) requests for favours or dispensations arising in the internal forum. The Datary's operation was a source of revenue for the papal treasury. By following a tariff system ("Composition"[19]) set up by Pope Sixtus IV a half century earlier, it managed to avoid any charge of simony. There followed, therefore, a long debate marked by an exchange of position papers and refutations between a majority who favoured the status quo but were willing to support the correction of certain abuses, and the minority, led by Contarini, who favoured radical adjustments to the system in place. The majority had the advantage of juridical expertise, combining a certain practical realism with a real lack of imagination, while the minority had a wider and more spiritual vision of the image that the Church should project. Without necessarily adhering to the utopian vision of a return to a pristine and virtuous Church, the minority was fully aware that the reproaches hurled by Protestants at the traditional Church had resonated with many Christians for twenty years, that they could not make that disappear completely, and that it was necessary to face the reproaches head on. Theirs was a realism of another kind altogether.

Faced with so much opposition Paul III finally sided with the majority who opposed implementing any of the recommendations of the *Consilium*. In his inertia, he seemed to justify the ironic parody of Psalm 148:5[20] expressed by Girolamo Seripando, the superior general of the Augustinians: *"Dixit et non fecit"* (He spoke and he did nothing).

19 Fees paid for a dispensation were considered alms offered to the Holy See.
20 The Psalm says of the Lord God, "He spoke and it was done."

Still, these debates and projects did not count for nothing when the Council of Trent once again set itself to look at the question of reforming the Church. The council Fathers – many of them the same persons who had already spoken out for the cause of reform – could call upon the pastoral and theological reflections which had been enunciated and advocated in the *Consilium de emendanda ecclesia*.

CHAPTER FIVE

Initiation of Reform

The admission of abuses and proposals for reform in the *Consilium* were clearly more honest and pertinent than the well-meaning but ineffective discourses of earlier years. In the period falling between the *Consilium* and the Council of Trent (1545–1563), the Catholic Church tried a number of other initiatives which could be considered as preludes to what It would attempt and ultimately accomplish at the Council of Trent. Some of these attempts led to nothing, but others sometimes yielded good results. This was the case with the meetings that took place between Catholics and Protestants in 1540–1541. They were known then as interconfessional conferences. We today might call them ecumenical dialogues.

Dialogue: An Apprenticeship or an Impossibility?

The dialogues took place at the initiative of a very concerned Emperor Charles V, for whom it was politically expedient to resolve the confessional divisions that had arisen among his German subjects. He needed, on the one hand, to remain faithful to the oath he had taken at his imperial coronation to protect the Catholic faith and, on the other, to preserve the unity of his Empire. As well, he was fully aware that continued procrastination by the papacy could cause untold danger to Christian Europe, since only a united Christendom could stand up to the very real menace of Turkish invasion. At this time he also believed that the settling of major theological differences between Catholics and Protestants would do more to bring about confessional concord than would correction of the abuses denounced by the Protestants. As we shall see, however, he would later change his mind and adopt the opposite position.

The failure of earlier, similar conferences held at Leipzig in 1534 and 1539 could be blamed on Rome's refusal to send official representatives to them. The colloquy that was convened in June 1540 at Speyer and later transferred (on account of the plague) to Haguenau in Alsace, and finally held in Worms in November, took place in the presence of two diplomats from the Holy See, Lorenzo Campeggio and Giovanni Morone. As is often the case, numerous procedural questions hindered the delegates from moving on to serious discussions. As well, the question of how to define the Church continued to divide the different parties. In the end, the colloquy delegated one Catholic, Johann Eck, and one Protestant, Philipp Melanchthon, to try to resolve differences on one single question: original sin.

In order to carry on the theological dialogues, the emperor called another conference, this one to be held at Regensburg in conjunction with the imperial Diet. The theologians were able to agree on a basis for discussion that they called "The Book of Regensburg." Its twenty-three articles, drawn up by the Catholic Johannes Gropper and the Protestant Martin Butzer, were supposed to be limited to points on which all could agree, but in reality it contained some points of divergence.

Pope Paul III did not really favour the emperor's initiative because he feared that the precedent of holding such a parley at the imperial Diet, where Lutherans and Catholics had equal status, might be looked on as a German national council. But he could not appear to oppose the search for religious unity. He therefore again delegated Giovanni Morone and, in May 1540, named Gasparo Contarini, who had played such a major role in drawing up the *Consilium de emendanda ecclesia*. Charles V welcomed this latter choice of a convinced partisan of reform.

When Contarini departed from Rome for Regensburg in March 1541, his instructions did not include his taking part in an ecumenical dialogue. As far as Rome was concerned he was simply to meet with "heretical" theologians to familiarize himself with their views – a kind of remote preparation for an eventual general council. This procedure was common practice in the history of the Church as the most apt way to deal with disputes involving matters of faith. Contarini therefore unexpectedly found himself in an infinitely complex situation, caught between two extreme positions, neither of which put much confidence in this type of meeting. He was obliged to give priority to issues which were primarily political – to points of contention between the emperor and the pope. It was the ultimate test of his diplomatic skills, knowledge, and civility.

The actual theological part of the colloquy took place from 28 April to 22 May 1541. It pitted the Protestants Melanchthon, Butzer,

Calvin, and Johannes Pistorius against Eck, Gropper, Julius Pflug, and Seripando. Contarini took no part personally in the discussions, but he met with the Catholic theologians in the presence of Morone and of Tommaso Badia, before and after each of their sessions.

No prospect of agreement on a common text concerning the Eucharist was possible, since the Protestants refused to allow the term "transubstantiation" to be included. A similar stalemate occurred concerning the authority and role of the Church to interpret Sacred Scripture. However, on 5 May the theologians of both sides were able to hammer out an agreement on Article 5 dealing with justification. Even though in the end it was not adopted officially by the Churches, this historic document has been dissected and analyzed by commentators both at that time and later. The terminology that had been agreed upon had no resonances with medieval scholasticism. Instead, it employed exclusively the biblical vocabulary of the Protestant side. The controversial issue of merit was never mentioned, and thus nobody was obliged either to affirm or to deny it.

On this key question of justification – how human beings arrive at salvation – everyone agreed that it was by the grace of Jesus Christ. But was there any role for man himself in this process? According to the Protestants, man's role was purely passive, because grace exercised an altogether overpowering "external imputation" on him. The Catholic position assigned human beings an active, if partial, role in their salvation, in that God's grace transformed the will of man. It set him free to choose between good and evil acts. The theologians of Regensburg tried to accommodate both positions by adopting what has been called "double justification," allowing in fact a two-stage process set in motion exclusively by the grace of Christ.

Neither Luther nor Rome accepted this ambiguous formulation. Contarini was criticized for accepting it, although the pope congratulated him in all other aspects of his legation. We can certainly see here a strong indication that confessional positions were hardening during the 1540s. Many observers already felt that the two sides were irreconcilable. Right up to the point of his death the following year, however, Contarini continued to defend the theology of double justification – so convinced was he that in no way did it fall short of Catholic doctrine. We shall see later that, when taken up by the Council of

Trent, this interpretation of the mysterious interplay of grace and free will would once again be rejected.

The Catholic theologians knew very well, however, that even if the doctrinal agreement had been ratified it would not suffice to resolve the crisis in the Church. Contarini wrote at the time, "Just as it is impossible to live in a house that has nothing but a foundation, so would nothing ever be right in the Church unless a thoroughgoing reform were put in place."[1] This should alert us, however, to the fact that the foundation of which he spoke was the doctrinal basis on which the disciplinary reforms would later be grounded. As we shall see in the following chapter, the combining or complementary adoption of dogmatic decrees and disciplinary reforms would be the key to most of what was accomplished in Trent.

It is significant that Contarini spent the last months of his life pleading for such reform and describing the means to accomplish it. In July he wrote to the bishops in the Empire, urging them to allow only trustworthy and experienced men to preach in their dioceses. He even wrote treatises to be used "as guides for preaching the Christian Gospel." Reflecting as a pastor he posed the question: how far should one go in preaching to the people such delicate and controversial questions like justification? He opted for omitting no part of Catholic doctrine from preaching, even when preaching to the people, but he also says that the main purpose of preaching should be to lead them to personal conversion and sorrow for sin.

The path of interconfessional dialogue therefore proved to be a limited means to reform. The failure of the Colloquy of Regensburg – or, in the opinion of others, its partial success – weighed very heavily on the way both sides would regard the Council of Trent, particularly when an invitation to attend the Council was extended to Protestants in 1553. When, twenty years later, a situation similar to what had taken place at Regensburg happened at the Colloquy of Poissy between French Catholics and Protestants, it moved the king of France to adopt a more favourable attitude to the Council of Trent.

---

1   Elisabeth G. Gleason, *Gasparo Contarini: Venice, Rome, and Reform* (Berkeley, Calif., 1993), 235.

The Initiatives

The council Fathers at Trent did not find themselves without models or precedents about how to renew the Church. From the first years of the sixteenth century there had been within the Catholic Church a number of specific, if unofficial, suggestions, initiatives, and innovations by advocates of reform that served later as inspiration for actions of the council. We can see already in the movement which Augustin Renaudet[2] called the "Pre-reform" the basic framework for the later program taken up at the Council of Trent.

Renewal by Returning to the Sources

From its very first sessions, as we shall later see, the Council of Trent turned its attention to the sources of divine revelation. Just as Protestant Reformers had done in their search for the pure word of God, the council implicitly took into account the considerable work done by humanist scholars on the Bible.

Some humanists had resorted to the approach taken by Origen in the third century when he produced his Hexaple Bible. In it Origen presented in adjacent columns the Hebrew and Greek versions of the Old Testament. The most successful revival of that approach in the sixteenth century was the Complutensian Polyglot Bible produced at the University of Alcalá under the inspiration and patronage of the Spanish Cardinal Francisco Ximénes de Cisneros.[3] After drawing up his plans in 1502, he gathered the necessary manuscripts and brought together the scholars required to accomplish his goal. It was ready for the press in 1514, but its six large folio volumes emerged from the press only in 1521. They contained the Old Testament printed in adjacent columns in Hebrew, Greek, and Latin and the New Testament in Greek and Latin. Some scholars considered its methodology to be too conservative, since it corrected the received texts only when the most ancient manuscripts authorized adopting a variant reading.

2   Renaudet, *Préréforme et humanisme à Paris pendant les premières guerres d'Italie (1494–1517)* (Paris, 1916; 2nd ed. 1953).
3   On his Polyglot Bible, see Jerry H. Bentley, *Humanists and Holy Writ: New Testament Scholarship in the Renaissance* (Princeton, N.J., 1983), 70–111.

At that same time, Jacques Lefèvre d'Étaples (c. 1450–1536), working alone first in Paris and then in Meaux under the patronage of Bishop Guillaume Briçonnet, published in 1509 an edition of the Psalms[4] which ranged, side-by-side, five different Latin versions. This allowed scholars to learn much about how certain phrases of the Bible had evolved through the centuries. He then began to prepare a new Latin version of the New Testament based on original texts. His editions of the Pauline Epistles, the Gospels, and the apostolic Epistles, accompanied by paraphrases, philological notes, and commentaries,[5] drew negative criticism from many Catholic theologians.[6] Despite such opposition and inspired by a pastoral ideal, Lefèvre enlisted the help of some "evangelical" disciples, and began in 1520 to translate the whole Bible into French – a work he completed in 1530.[7]

Erasmus of Rotterdam (1469–1536) was a leader in the effort to produce a better text of Sacred Scripture. His *Novum Instrumentum* (1516) contained the first printed Greek text of the New Testament along with the traditional Vulgate Latin and his own new Latin version. As later editions of it appeared, he made numerous changes and added prefaces in which he elaborated what he called "the philosophy of Christ." Although he strongly advocated translations of the Bible into vernacular languages, Erasmus contented himself with helping those charged with preaching the Word of God to understand it better. To this end he composed prolific annotations of the New Testament and paraphrases of all its books except the Apocalypse – all composed in his elegant Latin style.[8]

The Italian Dominican Sante Pagnini, a disciple of Savonarola, is not as well known as many of the other humanist scholars, but his

---

4   Guy Bedouelle, *Le Quincuplex psalterium de Lefèvre d'Étaples: Un guide de lecture* (Geneva, 1979).

5   For an English translation of Lefèvre's Preface to his *Commentaries on the Four Gospels*, see Olin, 107–17.

6   See Erika Rummel, ed., *Biblical Humanism and Scholasticism in the Age of Erasmus* (Leiden, 2008), which contains thirteen articles on scholastic objections to humanistic biblical exegesis.

7   Lefèvre's translation of the Bible was printed in Antwerp in 1530. French bibles could not be printed in France until after 1560.

8   The best synthetic study of Erasmus is by Cornelis Augustijn, *Erasmus: His Life, Works, and Influence*, trans. J.C. Grayson (Toronto; Buffalo, 1991).

work on the Bible yielded one of the most accurate textual foundations on which later translations and commentaries were based. Like John Colet[9] in London, Pagnini's scriptural lectures in the priory of San Marco in Florence emphasized the literal sense of the text. His Latin Bible, based on his study of Hebrew and Greek texts and published in 1528 in Lyons, is accompanied by a number of philological and historical appendices which were essential tools used by all biblical scholars of the sixteenth century.

Other groups who looked to a return to the sources were monks, friars, and other religious communities seeking to reform monastic and religious life. More specifically they called for a greater fidelity to the charisms of their founders. That was certainly what had motivated Girolamo Savonarola as he worked tirelessly to join together a reform of the Dominican Order with a prophetic, sometimes violent call for a reform of the whole Roman Church. He succeeded in returning the friars of San Marco in Florence to a life of strict poverty and asceticism, as the founder Dominic had wished. Despite his condemnation and execution, Savonarola's spirited reform led Pagnini and many others to regard him as a saint. An undying Savonarolan spirit marked many advocates of the reform of Catholicism, primarily in Italy but also in Spain. It affected not only Dominican friars and sisters but also the society in which they worked.

In France, although the works of Savonarola were published and circulated in Paris early in the sixteenth century,[10] the reform of the Dominican Order actually came about from the Dutch Dominican Congregation.[11] Jean Clérée, the confessor of King Louis XII, was one of the leading agents of this reform. He fought to integrate the French Dominican priories in Troyes, Tours, and most especially the Paris priory of Saint-Jacques into the reformed Dutch Congregation. The resistance of some individual friars and even entire priories was so

9   See Colet's Convocation Sermon (1512) in Olin, 27–39.
10 Savonarola's *Expositio super Miserere*, a commentary on Psalm 50, appeared in 1502. A larger collection, *Expositio in psalmos [et alia opera]* was printed c. 1508. See Brigitte Moreau, *Inventaire chronologique des éditions parisiennes du XVIe siècle*, vol. 1: *1501–1510* (Paris, 1972), 87, no. 116; 297, no. 176.
11 It is known in French history as the "Congrégation de Hollande."

obstinate, however, that some cases had to be resolved in the Parlement of Paris or even by order of the king.

Reformers who were Augustinian Canons Regular took their inspiration from the *devotio moderna*, as did the Flemish scholar and college reformer Jan Standonck. After serving a term as rector of the University of Paris in 1486, Standonck became the principal of the Collège de Montaigu. His reform of the curriculum and of discipline there was criticized bitterly by Erasmus, who spent one year under Standonck's direction. But it helped promote a more general implementation of reforms in the university. Standonck's career is emblematic of the wide-ranging influence of the Brethren of the Common Life on many reforming spirits.

In the same way, many of the monastic orders joined the movement of return to the sources by working for a more strict observance of the Rule. An outstanding example in Italy was the Benedictine Congregation of Santa Giustina of Padua.[12] Its reformed *Constitutions* served as a model for renewal in other abbeys. One of the main targets of the reformers, from which many abuses stemmed, was the appointment of abbots for life, especially if they were commendatory abbots, i.e. not members of the abbey or its order. The reformers wanted elections every three years, with the option of renewing the appointment. Canonical visitors were charged with maintaining the discipline outlined in the Rule, especially pertaining to anything that hindered stability, such as prolonged sojourns at universities.

That does not imply, however, that monastic reformers were hostile to study and the intellectual life. On the contrary, many humanist scholars returned to their cloisters. In France a notable example of reformed Benedictine observance was the Congregation of Chezal-Benoist. Although not without some resistance, the great abbey of Saint-Germain-des-Prés joined it, as did the abbeys of Cluny, Cîteaux, and even the Grande Chartreuse.

Thus, between 1485 and 1515 a whole generation of reforming spirits had experienced notable success in the renewal of existing

12 On the reform there see Barry Collett, *Italian Benedictine Scholars and the Reformation: The Congregation of Santa Giustina of Padua* (Oxford; New York, 1985).

religious orders.[13] Ten or twenty years later, another option came into play: the creation of new forms and groups of religious life that were specifically adapted to the needs of the time. Usually less strict than the older orders, they were thus more able to take up a wider range of pastoral apostolates. This was the case of the Theatines, who were founded in 1524 in Rome jointly by Gaetano de Thiene (1480–1547) and by Gian Pietro Carafa (the future Pope Paul IV), who at the time was bishop of the diocese of Chieti (Theate) from which the new order took its name. Although the Theatines undertook the canonical vow of poverty and the statute of common life, they worked closely with the secular clergy. Their foundation was one of the first to join pastoral work to the exigencies of canonical religious life.[14]

In 1529 Matteo di Bassi of Urbino founded a new branch of the great Franciscan Order. His Capuchins, bearded and wearing a hood and sandals, became symbols of a return to a pristine fervor and of zeal for Catholic reform,[15] although they had to survive a great crisis when Bernardino Ochino, their vicar-general, went over to Protestantism in 1541.

On 15 August 1534, on the heights of Montmartre north of Paris, Ignatius of Loyola (1491–1556), having already travelled a complex and paradoxical life path, committed himself, along with six companions, to a life of service to the Church. In 1540, Pope Paul III issued the bull *Regimini militantis ecclesiae*[16] that recognized the Society of Jesus as a new religious order in the Church. In 1540, the companions made a certain number of decisions which gave to the new Society a fundamental character. The most obvious and determining of these was their engaging in a more exacting and fixed ministry than what the objectives of all earlier religious orders had prescribed.[17]

We will encounter Capuchins and Jesuits in much of the rest of this book. Some of them will be canonized saints, others not; but they

13 See Jean-Marie Le Gall, *Les moines au temps des réformes: France (1480–1560)* (Seyssel [Haute-Savoie], 2001).
14 For an English translation of the Theatine Rule (1526), see Olin, 128–32.
15 For an English translation of the Capuchin Constitutions of 1536, see Olin, 149–81.
16 For an English translation of *Regimini militantis ecclesiae*, see Olin, 198–204.
17 John W. O'Malley, *The First Jesuits* (Cambridge, Mass., 1993).

will be among the leading personalities of the reform of Catholicism as they put into action this grand design of renewal for which their Orders had been created – and this to such a degree that they will sometimes be identified not only with its triumphs but also with its failures and its excesses.

The Growth of Printing and the Reform of Education

It would not be correct to suggest that the Church had to wait for the age of humanism and its innovative pedagogical methods before beginning to organize and promote the instruction of children and adults in their faith. But it is true that the invention and rapid expansion of printing, by changing the way knowledge was transmitted, greatly enlarged the scope of such instruction. One should not try to compare, for example, the relatively small number of literate persons in the pre-Gutenberg era with the greatly expanded numbers two centuries later. In the first instance, only a relatively few manuscripts of a text such as Jean Gerson's *ABC des simples gens*[18] or similar manuals composed to teach the rudiments of literacy and catechism could be copied by hand; they were prohibitively expensive to most people. In the second instance, the same text (and numerous others) could be produced in hundreds or thousands of copies at a fraction of the cost.

Following the example of Erasmus and Juan Luis Vives, the Protestant reformers – in particular Philipp Melanchthon, who was known as the "schoolmaster of Germany" – placed strong emphasis on educating children in schools. This included teaching them the rudiments of the Christian faith. Catechisms for the masses, whether in small or large format, no matter what their name, were first developed by Luther, Zwingli, Butzer, and Calvin.

The Catholic Bishop Jacopo Sadoleto of the southern French diocese of Carpentras corresponded with Melanchthon and Calvin. He published in 1533 a treatise on education affirming the possibility of

---

18 See Gerson, *Oeuvres complètes*, ed. Palémon Glorieux (Paris, 1960–), 7: 154–7, no. 310. A work of only four printed pages, it contains the major prayers, the Credo, lists of virtues and vices, the Beatitudes, the spiritual and corporal works of mercy, and other elements of spiritual and moral instruction.

helping children discover their "naturally Christian" souls. He confides the first steps in this education to the fathers of families, and he encourages them to let joy and liberty prevail in the home.[19]

The Jesuits were to become the accomplished masters of Christian education, and that ambition was present from the early years of the Society. The founding of the Collegio San Niccolò in Messina, Sicily, presumed that "the students must profit spiritually from the teaching of Christian doctrine, from sermons, and from encouragement."

Catechetical instruction held a prominent place in Jesuit pedagogy. On 13 August 1554, after hearing from Peter Canisius about the level of ignorance of German children, Ignatius of Loyola wrote back to him that children and illiterate (*pueri et rudes*) needed a short handbook of Catholic doctrine. He added, however, that the clergy needed more extended doctrinal texts and that the better educated people needed "a summa of theology." Between 1555 and 1558 Canisius managed to publish the short handbook for children, the texts for the clergy, and the "summa" for the literate people that Ignatius had recommended. The collection of texts aimed at the clergy was the most successful of the three, becoming known eventually simply as "the Canisius."[20]

Several reforming prelates also undertook new catechetical approaches, each following his particular interest and talent. Already in 1542 (the year of his death) Gasparo Contarini had written a *Catechesis*, or Christian Instruction, which consisted of forty-one questions and answers on the most controversial points of doctrine. In 1558, the newly-appointed Dominican archbishop of Toledo, Bartolomé de Carranza de Miranda (1503–1576), who had already shown remarkable zeal in his work in England and in the Low Countries, composed a long book that he entitled *Commentaries on Christian Catechism*. He

19 *De pueris recte instituendis* (Venice, 1533). See the English edition and translation in *Sadoleto on Education: A Translation of the De pueris recte instituendis,* ed. and trans. Ernest T. Campagnac and Kenneth Forbes (London; New York, 1916).

20 It was printed more than 200 times during his lifetime alone. His *Institutiones, et Exercitamentas christianae pietatis* (Antwerp, 1566), combining the *Catechism* for the middle grades and his *Lectiones et Precationes ecclesiasticæ* (Ingolstadt, 1556), was also reprinted many times in Rome and elsewhere.

organized it according to the fundamental structure of such catechisms: the Creed, the Ten Commandments, the sacraments, and the
"Our Father." Written in Castilian Spanish, it was a learned theological treatise intended for Catholics living in a Protestant milieu. It
drew fire, however, from critics who said it was influenced by
Erasmus and the *alumbrados* ("enlightened ones"), a term given to a
spirituality considered at that time to be heterodox. As a result,
Carranza was subjected to a seventeen-year-long series of actions in
court brought by his enemies, although the controversy was finally
ended with an ambiguous settlement which satisfied neither side.

This was partly due to the existence of two of the other agencies
already at work prior to the Council of Trent: the Inquisition and the
Index. Both oriented the reform of Catholicism towards a Counter-
Reformation posture. The Spanish Inquisition had been instigated at
the end of the fifteenth century prior to the advent of Protestantism.
It was only in 1542, with the creation of a special commission of
cardinals, that the first signs of what would become the Roman
Inquisition appeared. It would only later take on a more focused
function when its most influential member, Cardinal Gian Pietro
Carafa, whom we saw earlier as a co-founder of the Theatines, became Pope Paul IV (1555–1559). Carafa was also the one who, in 1557,
gave the order to draw up the first papal Index of Prohibited Books. It
appeared two years later.[21] It drew upon earlier catalogues of prohibited books issued in Paris (1544–1555), Louvain (1548), Venice
(1549), and other Catholic centres,[22] but it reorganized and rational-
ized those lists and also added new authors and titles to the ones pro-
scribed by Paris and Louvain. It was roundly perceived to be too
severe in its judgments, and thus underwent a thorough revision in
1561. The Council of Trent was to order still another revision to bring
it up to date. The Roman Church sought through this means to inhibit
the spread of Protestant literature and to harness the tremendous

---

21 *Index des livres interdits*, ed. J.M. De Bujanda et al. (Sherbrooke, Québec;
    Geneva, 1984–2002). See vol. 8, *Index de Rome, 1557, 1559, 1564: les premiers
    index romains et l'index du Concile de Trente.* Vol. 9 contains the three later
    Roman indexes that were issued in the sixteenth century.
22 See the series *Index des livres interdits* (preceding note).

influence of the rapidly expanding book trade in the service of a balanced and effective reform of Catholicism.

Reforming Bishops and Their Pastoral Ideals

Years before the Council of Trent opened, certain bishops were successfully promoting the pastoral ideals they found in the patristic texts and other writings that humanist scholars had made available. Some may have found that ideal in Erasmus' letter to Paul Volz, which served as a preface to a new edition (1518) of his *Handbook of the Christian Soldier*, in which he wrote, "The honorable role of bishops is to come as close as possible to the virtues of Christ and his apostles." Like many others he considered the parable of the Good Shepherd "who gives his life for his sheep" to be the best example of how a bishop might achieve this ideal.[23] As we have already seen, two years earlier (1516), while still a young layman, Gasparo Contarini composed a treatise *On the Office of Bishop* that proposed the highest standards of pastoral care for bishops.[24]

We have chosen to describe briefly the actions of three of these "pre-reform" Catholic bishops who, between 1520 and 1545, exercised their ministries in three different countries and in very different ways. The three are Guillaume Briçonnet, bishop of Meaux in France, John Fisher, bishop of Rochester in England, and Gian Matteo Giberti, bishop of Verona in Italy. We might have chosen others in Spain or the Englishman Reginald Pole, who was the archbishop of Canterbury during the short return of that kingdom to Roman Catholicism (1553–1558).[25] Although not very numerous, they and others like them often left a lasting impact on the religious character of the dioceses where they ministered.

Guillaume Briçonnet (1470–1534) was born into an important family of financiers, statesmen, and prelates. His father, who became a priest after his wife died, was the bishop of Saint-Malo and became a cardinal of the Church. There were two particularly

---

23 English translation and annotation by Charles Fantazzi in *Collected Works of Erasmus* (Toronto, 1988) 66: 1–127.

24 See above, p. 40 n7.

25 Thomas F. Mayer, *Reginald Pole: Prince and Prophet* (Cambridge, 2000).

important influences on Guillaume Briçonnet's life. The first was his teacher, Josse Clichtove (1472–1543), Flemish doctor of theology in Paris and graduate of the Collège de Sorbonne, who wrote prolifically and inculcated into his students an authentic priestly and liturgical spirituality.[26] The second influence was Marguerite d'Angoulême, the sister of King Francis I and future queen of Navarre. In reading the spiritual correspondence exchanged between Briçonnet and Marguerite, which lasted from 1521 to 1524,[27] one cannot always distinguish who is the spiritual director of whom. Both these influences moved Briçonnet to think and work as a humanist and evangelical bishop. He was named commendatory abbot of Saint-Germain-des-Prés, and from that position he became the patron of Jacques Lefèvre d'Étaples. As bishop of Lodève and then of Meaux (1515), he resolved to promote reform in his diocese by a greater use of the Bible to enrich the spirituality and change the method of preaching of his priests. In 1521, he placed this program of renewal in the diocese of Meaux under the direction of Lefèvre d'Étaples and several of his disciples. The preaching of some of them, in the opinion of the Faculty of Theology of Paris, smacked of "Lutheranism" – a generic term at that time for all forms of heterodox thinking – and led to condemnation by the Faculty. A number of "Lutheran" incidents in Meaux led to investigations and prosecution before the Parlement of Paris in 1525. Some persons convicted of heresy were executed, and others considered suspect were silenced.[28]

26 For a short sketch of his career in English, see James K. Farge, *Biographical Register of Paris Doctors of Theology, 1500–1536* (Toronto, 1980), 90–104, no. 101. For the definitive study, see Jean-Pierre Massaut, *Josse Clichtove, l'humanisme, et la réforme du clergé* (Paris, 1968).

27 Guillaume Briçonnet and Marguerite d'Angoulême, *Correspondance, 1521–1524*, ed. Christine Martineau and Michel Veissière, with the assistance of Henry Heller (Geneva, 1975–1979).

28 See James K. Farge, *Orthodoxy and Reform in Early Reformation France: The Faculty of Theology of Paris, 1500–1543* (Leiden, 1985), 169–86.

Michel Veissière, the biographer of Briçonnet,[29] has shown how, despite the troubling presence of "Lutherans" and other adherents of the "new faith" after 1525, Briçonnet was able to continue his pastoral activities in ways that the Council of Trent would ratify and even legislate. He resided in his diocese, he carried out pastoral visitations, he watched over the quality and the orthodoxy of preaching, and he was particularly vigilant about convening diocesan synods that would help his Catholic reforms take root. He participated in the provincial Council of Sens, convened in October 1528 by Guillaume Duprat, the cardinal-archbishop of Sens, to consider doctrinal issues and disciplinary measures. Its forty-one decrees on doctrine and morals[30] anticipated by more than thirty years, even in many of their details, the approaches and principal decisions that would be taken at Trent.[31] Briçonnet's institution in 1527 of a solemn procession of the Blessed Sacrament is symbolic of his strong attachment to Catholicism. Neither a hero nor a saint, Briçonnet showed from 1525 to his death in 1534 the determination of a diocesan bishop to bring about reform from within the Roman Church.

Our second reformist prelate, John Fisher (1460–1535), bishop of Rochester, fell victim to the divorce question and resulting political strife between King Henry VIII and Pope Clement VII. Most of Fisher's biographers[32] have highlighted his involvement with the University of Cambridge, where he was chancellor beginning in 1504. They have also elaborated upon his intellectual activity which ranged from his involvement with humanists – friendly in the case of Erasmus, more polemical vis-à-vis Lefèvre d'Étaples – to his defense

29 Veissière, *L'évêque Guillaume Briçonnet (1470–1534): Contribution à la connaissance de la réforme catholique à la veille du Concile de Trente* (Provins [Seine-et-Marne], 1986).

30 *Decreta prouincialis Concilii Senonensis* ... (Paris, 1529). The council's decrees were drawn up by Briçonnet's mentor, Josse Clichtove (see above, p. 60 n26).

31 Hubert Jedin, *L'évêque dans la tradition pastorale du XVIe siècle*, trans. and extended by Paul Broutin (Bruges, 1953).

32 See in particular Brendan Bradshaw and Eamon Duffy, eds., *Humanism, Reform, and the Reformation: The Career of Bishop John Fisher* (Cambridge; New York, 1989) and Richard Rex, *The Theology of John Fisher* (Cambridge; New York, 1991).

of orthodoxy against the Protestant Reformers. With good reason they have concentrated on his defense of the validity of King Henry VIII's marriage to Catherine of Aragon.

King Henry VII, wishing to please his mother Lady Margaret Beaufort, had named Fisher bishop of Rochester in 1504. It was one of the poorest dioceses in England. The diocesan registers, all extant, allow us to form a picture of how this learned prelate administered his diocese. Even though he had responsibilities at Cambridge and at court, and partly because of his health, Fisher resided in Rochester. He made pastoral visitations of the whole diocese every three years, with the exception of periods when his membership in Parliament impeded him, and he regularly participated in diocesan and provincial synods. He watched over the personal and theological formation of his priests, and did not hesitate to send them back to school to raise them to the standard he held. But it was primarily in his approach to preaching that one can perceive how he joined theological and mystical learning with exhortations to his flock about their spiritual and moral reform. His sermons, which were published during his lifetime, reveal a markedly medieval spirituality that stressed Purgatory and called for spiritual conversion by close observance of the commandments of God and of the Church.[33] In 1535 Pope Paul III named him a cardinal of the Church, but just three weeks later, on 22 June 1535, he was beheaded for refusing to take the oath recognizing Henry VIII as supreme head of the Church in England. His execution preceded by only a month that of the great English humanist and chancellor of England, Thomas More, who was beheaded for the same reason.

Gian Matteo Giberti (1495–1543) was born out-of-wedlock to a Genoese admiral. He was legitimized in 1514 by Pope Leo X, and proceeded to have a brilliant ecclesiastical career. Ludwig von Pastor considered him to be the animating spirit of all that was good in

---

33 See *The English Works of John Fisher, Bishop of Rochester: Sermons and Other Writings, 1520 to 1535*, ed. Cecilia A. Hatt (Oxford; New York, 2002). See also *The English Works of John Fisher*, ed. John E.B. Mayor (London, 1876; repr. Millwood, N.Y., 1976).

Rome.[34] Named bishop of Verona in 1524, Giberti was one of the main architects of Pope Clement VII's pro-French foreign policy that led to the catastrophic Sack of Rome by imperial forces in 1527. Prior to this time he had not neglected his diocese, but he now withdrew to it and remained there until his death. Beginning in 1528, he could be seen as one of the most active and imaginative Catholic reformers.[35] As a friend and defender of Erasmus, Giberti's actions showed markedly humanistic traits. For example, he installed in his own palace a printing press that produced both patristic and modern texts in Greek. The formation of future priests was a priority with him, and his "school for acolytes" gave them instruction in both secular and religious subjects.

Giberti's mixture of practical knowledge and theological learning, the pastoral visitations that he conducted systematically, and his work with the reform Commission that produced the *Consilium de emendanda ecclesia*,[36] all show him to have been an exemplary bishop. He was consciously imitated by Charles Borromeo, who derived his knowledge of Giberti vicariously from two of Giberti's collaborators, Niccolò Ormaneto and Agostino Valier. Giberti is the acknowledged inspiration and model for the concept of the ideal bishop which emerged from the decree on the sacrament of Holy Orders promulgated at the Council of Trent on 15 July 1563.

34 For Pastor's eloquent praise of Giberti, see Pastor, *The History of the Popes: from the Close of the Middle Ages, Drawn from the Secret Archives of the Vatican and other Original Sources,* ed. and trans. F.I. Antrobus et al. (London; St Louis, Mo., 1891–1961), 10: 424–42.
35 For an English translation of Giberti's *Constitutions* for his diocese and clergy, see Olin, 133–48.
36 See above, pp. 41–6.

CHAPTER SIX

The Key to Reform

Three different papal bulls of convocation were required before the Council of Trent was finally able to assemble. The political situation in Europe was the major cause of the delay, but it was also due to different ideas of how the council should proceed. In each bull the pope set forth three similar goals that he enumerated in the same order, although important nuances can be discerned in the way each text was formulated. The first of the three bulls, *Ad Dominici gregis curam* of 2 June 1536,[1] called for the council to meet at Mantua in May 1537, and assigned it three tasks: the extirpation of heresies and errors, the correction of the morals of the Christian people, and the establishment of universal peace. This latter task actually called for a Crusade against the infidels.

In a similar way, the 22 May 1542 bull, *Initio nostri huius pontificatus,*[2] calling for a council to assemble in Trent, proposed to restore "the integrity of Christian faith ... to return to a higher moral standard and to eradicate the evils" that afflicted the Church. Finally, in his bull *Laetare Jerusalem* of 19 November 1544,[3] once more setting Trent as the point of assembly, Paul III directed the council to suppress religious differences, to reform the moral life of Christian people, and to come to the aid of Christians living in regions ruled by infidels. The only thing new in this third, successful bull of convocation was that the third goal called for a joint Crusade of all Christian princes – an alliance which would not only free Christians from the rule of infidels

---

1   It called for the council to gather at Mantua in May 1537. Mansi 35: 359–62 dates this bull to 4 June. See also *Bullarum privilegiorum ac diplomatum Romanorum pontificum amplissima collectio*, ed. Charles Cocquelines (Rome, 1745), 4.1: 143–5.

2   Ibid., 207–11. Not in Mansi.

3   Mansi 35: 375–8. Not in the *Bullarum privilegiorum*, which gives no documentation for the final four years of Paul III's papacy.

but would also force the warring Christian princes to make peace among themselves.

If the Council of Trent were to be more effective than the Fifth Lateran Council, it was essential to have in place a definite agenda and a program for post-conciliar implementation of its decisions. Just as essential, because of the enormity of the task, was the need to start off on the right foot. Here is where differences of opinion almost sealed the fate of the council. The pope and the Roman Curia believed that the council's order of business should follow the one set forth in the bull of convocation. They maintained that the tradition established by ecumenical councils through the centuries required that attention be given first to matters of doctrine. Rome was motivated in this by two overriding reasons. First, it feared a renewal of the conciliarism that had followed the councils of Constance and Basel in the fifteenth century and had led to what was regarded as prolonged and unwarranted intervention of those councils in the life of the Church. Both the pope and the Curia wanted to safeguard the governing role of the papacy and to prevent the impending council from meddling in problems of discipline that were better left to the ordinary bureaucracy of the Church. Second, Rome feared that any delay in reaffirming the ultimate truth of Catholic doctrine might motivate the theologians to try to decide such questions on their own, and that their conclusions might be ratified by other assemblies such as the imperial Diet. That is what had been attempted at the Regensburg Colloquy in 1541, and it had proved troublesome to the papal magisterium.

The emperor and his counsellors, however – contrary to the views they had held prior to that colloquy – now proposed different priorities for Trent. They believed that the council should deal first of all with a thorough reform of the morals of the clergy and the people. This, they now proposed, would be the best way to address the objections of the Protestants. This same concern moved them, during a prolonged adjournment of the council, to institute the so-called Interim of Augsburg (1548) which granted dispensations in disciplinary matters like clerical celibacy and communion under both species. Charles V feared that the council's neglect of disciplinary issues was an affront to Protestant subjects and would split the Empire even more.

The ecclesiastical, diplomatic, and political stakes riding on these different views about what had caused the Protestant revolt and how best to deal with it were extremely high. It should therefore be no surprise that this debate on the council's order of business took up the first five weeks of the Council of Trent (13 December 1545 to 22 January 1546). It is an issue that is worth examining in more detail, because the solution that broke the deadlock made the Catholic Reformation not only possible but truly workable.

Cornelio Musso, the Franciscan bishop of Bitonto, gave the opening address to what was only a modest assembly of prelates on 13 December 1545. Like its precedent delivered by Giles of Viterbo at Lateran V,[4] it was a rhetorical but severe assessment of the state of the Catholic Church. Its principal thrust was about the resolution of doctrinal matters, especially "the dignity of the sacraments"; but it did not minimize the need to reform the morality "of the clergy, of kings, of princes, and of the people."[5]

In the first sessions that followed, the question was put in complete simplicity: "Should we begin with dogmas of faith or with disciplinary reforms?"[6] Serious discussion began on 18 January 1546. The debates between the two sides – the imperial delegates advocating priority to discipline and the papal delegates in favour of priority to dogma – were conducted vigorously but with courtesy.

Cristoforo Madruzzo, the bishop of Trent, convinced that abuses in the Church prompted the Lutherans to set up their erroneous doctrine, argued that primacy must be given to reform of discipline. He proposed that the council issue a friendly and fraternal invitation to them rather than launch into debates about doctrine. Curiously, he cited Acts 1:1 ("I wrote of all that Jesus did and taught") to back up his argument.[7]

Speakers who favoured the papal position, and especially the papal legates to the council, continued to stress the wisdom of earlier councils in taking up dogmatic questions first. Some among them argued that

4   See above, pp. 19–20.
5   *CT* 4: 525.
6   *CT* 4: 534.
7   *CT* 4: 567.

the reformation of morality would take so long to decide and implement that it would paralyze effective action of the council and thus nullify any beneficent effect on the Protestants. All the speakers, however, could acknowledge that, in fact, affirmation of dogma and reformation of morality were intimately tied one to the other.

One of the most interesting interventions was made by the legate Reginald Pole. He argued that the council must firmly restore solid doctrine or, as he put it, must restore "religion." Without that, he said, it would be impossible to do anything about reform of discipline. Pole repeatedly urged the council Fathers to follow the injunction of Christ, "Go out into the whole world and announce the Good News to all of creation" (Mk 16:15). Jesus did not say, "Go out and change the way men act!" Pole's very use of the word *religio,* a term dear to humanists, reveals a way of thinking which conceived of the faith not as a catalogue of truths but as an attitude of respectful meditation on the revealed Word of God. In this way Pole could say, "Wherever religion is truly integral, there can be no evil morals."[8] It was one step towards a resolution.

But the instructions of Pope Paul III, delivered in his name by his nephew Cardinal Alessandro Farnese, were unyielding. Each time the legates reported any suspicion that the majority of council Fathers wanted to begin with reform of discipline, arguing that heresy began because of abuses, the answer would come back from Rome that the agenda must maintain the priority of doctrine and only secondarily deal with disciplinary matters.[9]

Gradually, however, the idea began to gain ground that both doctrine and discipline must be dealt with at the same time. This was argued first and most strongly by Cardinal Lorenzo Campeggio. He insisted that, according to the Protestants with whom he was acquainted, the problems of faith and of morals were too closely linked to be treated separately. He added, however, that for them the disciplinary questions were of little importance or even indifferent (*adiaphora*).[10] Paul III finally began to yield. Not wishing to be seen

8   *CT* 4: 571.
9   *CT* 11.1: 291.
10   *CT* 4: 569.

as impeding the council's work, he conceded that both dogma and discipline could be considered at the same time; but he insisted that the debates about dogmas must have pride of place. Doctrine, he said, "is the very principle of the reform." The council Fathers were thus to enter by "the narrow gate" of dogma in order to arrive at a true reform of the Church in matters of both faith and morals. Most of the delegates were ready to obey. In their formal debates and informal conversations, legates and bishops had come to realize that many were skeptical of achieving any reform at all.[11] Thus, it became easier to agree that doctrine and discipline be discussed simultaneously. This was more than a compromise: it was a veritable decision. On 22 January 1546, the chief legate, Cardinal Giovanni Maria del Monte, astutely presented an agenda in which definitions of faith and matters of discipline would be considered conjointly – but in that order. The majority of the delegates present accepted the idea. More specifically, the council would issue two decrees on each question: the first on doctrine, the second on the abuses which had arisen in connection with the matter of faith under discussion. This solution also had the great advantage of not isolating canon law from its foundation in theology. Whereas Luther had rejected canon law, the Council of Trent rehabilitated it by showing how it is in useful harmony with the mission of the Church.

The solution arrived at on that day was still only a theoretical one, but it was to be regularly put into practice – even if, as we shall see, it could not be done in an absolutely systematic way. No one had realistically imagined that each issue or word in dealing with a point of doctrine would be treated in tandem with an issue or word relating to the reforms connected to it. In fact, as Pope Paul III had wished, the accent was first on points of dogma and then, in the course of later discussions, on the related "general reformation." The French bishops were not present for these debates about the agenda, but most of them concurred when they belatedly rejoined the council.

The historian has good reason to conclude that this two-fold approach endowed the council with a pragmatic and forceful plan of action. When previous councils had in like manner dealt with both

11   *CT* 11.1: 326.

dogma and discipline, they had lacked this strategic internal linking of the two that the Council of Trent had just instituted. More than merely a political compromise or a commonsensible solution, it was in fact the key that made possible the reform of the Catholic Church.

CHAPTER SEVEN

Reform by Council

The choice of Trent as the site for the council was a compromise between the pope and the emperor. Charles V, who was wary of increasing the protests and anxieties of his Protestant subjects, accepted Trent because it was an imperial city. Pope Paul III accepted it because it was an Italian-speaking city located south of the Alps.

The scope of this book does not include a presentation of the discussions and debates that took place at the Council of Trent. Other studies, both old and new, have already provided that to different degrees. We shall therefore limit ourselves in this chapter to seeing how the council Fathers implemented their decision to consider both doctrinal and disciplinary decrees at the same time. The example we have chosen for this is the most characteristic and most controversial of all the issues: the obligation of bishops to reside in their dioceses.

The Three Phases of the Council: 1545–1547, 1551–1552, 1562–1563

The council opened in Trent on 13 December 1545 in a very modest way, since only thirty-four delegates (twenty-nine cardinals and bishops and five abbots or superiors general) were present. By the seventh session (3 March 1547) the number of delegates present and voting had increased to seventy-one. As agreed, the debates began about doctrinal matters that had been challenged by the Reformers – issues such as Revelation (Scripture and Tradition), original sin, justification, Baptism, and Confirmation. Heeding the decision taken on 22 January 1546, the council Fathers were also looking to bring about a pastoral reformation that would help put an end to abuses in the Church. In March 1547 the papal legates, however, wanted to move the council to Bologna. Their pretext was fear of a plague at Trent, but in reality they believed that Trent provided a venue for Germany to exercise undue influence on the proceedings. When fourteen imperial delegates refused to move, the menacing shadow of schismatic conciliarism was cast over the council. Although this threat did not materialize, the council was suspended temporarily in September as a compromise measure.

The second phase of the council, convened five years later by Pope Julius III (Giovanni Maria del Monte) for a short period in 1551–1552, concerned itself once again with matters of doctrine that had been contested by the Protestants – particularly the Eucharist and the sacrament of Penance. The French king Henry II forbade attendance of French prelates during this session, because he was in political conflict with the pope. Most of the Spanish and German prelates, however, were present. The maximum number of delegates during this second phase – sixty-five voting members – was reached in the fourteenth session. Very few definitive texts were voted upon, but the theological advisors (*periti*) laid the groundwork for a number of projects that would be taken up in future sessions. This second phase is also notable for its reception of Protestant delegations, notably from Würtemberg. They were allowed to present their creedal statements, but the council did not allow discussion of them. It once again had to be suspended, this time on account of a number of military victories against the emperor achieved by the Schmalkaldic League of Protestant princes.

This second suspension lasted ten years. In its midst stood the pontificate of Paul IV (1555–1559),[1] who was strongly dedicated to reforming the Roman Curia and the diocese of Rome itself before even looking at renewal in the universal Church. It was the time of the most radical use of the Roman Inquisition. The year of his coronation, 1555, was also a watershed year for the entire political and religious situation in Europe. Charles V's abdication took place in that year, as did the Peace of Augsburg, which legalized and seemed to consecrate the confessional Churches in Germany. Reconvening the council in all those complex circumstances was impossible.

The treaties signed at Cateau-Cambrésis in April 1559 between France, Spain, and England opened up a short window of peace and of possibilities. Both Pope Pius IV (1559–1565) and his nephew Charles Borromeo, who was also his Secretary of State, believed the time was ripe to bring to completion the council's earlier work.

---

1   See above, p. 40, and below, pp. 85 and 88.

Emperor Ferdinand and the French monarchy thought a new council should start from scratch, but they did not prevail. The mood in the third phase of the Council of Trent was less one of reacting against Protestantism, as it had been in the first two phases, and more one of achieving a lasting renewal of Catholicism. Theologically there was an attempt to complete a comprehensive theology of all the sacraments, especially the sacrament of Holy Orders. What was achieved instead was a set of disciplinary measures to change the way candidates for this sacrament would be selected and trained. Seminaries were to be put in place, and texts were approved which boldly spelled out in great detail the rights and the responsibilities of bishops and parish priests – especially their obligation to reside in their dioceses and parishes.

The delegation of French bishops, led by Charles de Guise, Cardinal of Lorraine, arrived quite late. At the twenty-fourth session (11 November 1563) the number of voting delegates achieved its maximum total of two hundred thirty-two. But the time to conclude the council was drawing near. Once again all sorts of tensions came to the fore, and much remained to be done. The last sessions dealt with controversial theological and disciplinary questions such as the sacrament of Matrimony, devotion to the saints, and the doctrine of Purgatory.

The council finally dissolved itself on 4 December 1563. Since many details had not been worked out, it entrusted to the pope and the bishops the task of implementing the reforms it had mandated. As we shall see, this gave them – especially the pope – remarkable scope of action in the reform of Catholicism.

In order to have a better understanding of how the relation between dogmas and disciplinary reforms was worked out, we have inserted below a short chronological sketch of the sessions which approved the council's different decrees.[2] The canons are the more

---

2   For the Latin texts with facing English translations, see Norman P. Tanner, SJ, *Decrees of the Ecumenical Councils* (London; Washington, D.C., 1990). (= Tanner, *Decrees.*)

    For an older English translation see *Canons and Decrees of the Council of Trent,* ed. and trans. Henry Joseph Schroeder (St Louis, Mo.; London, 1941; repr. Rockford, Ill., 1978). (= *Canons and Decrees.*)

important of the two texts, since observance of them became obligatory for all Catholics. The council Fathers took great care in formulating them and setting forth the strict rules for their interpretation.

FOURTH SESSION (8 April 1546) (Tanner, *Decrees* 2: *663–5).
  Doctrine: Sacred Scripture and apostolic Traditions
  Reform: the Vulgate; the printing of sacred texts; use of vernacular languages

FIFTH SESSION (17 June 1546) (Tanner, *Decrees* 2: *665–70).
  Doctrine: Original sin
  Reform: Teaching and Preaching of the Scriptures

SIXTH SESSION (13 January 1547) (Tanner, *Decrees* 2: *671–*783).
  Doctrine: Justification
  Reform: the Residence of bishops and priests

SEVENTH SESSION (3 March 1547) (Tanner, *Decrees* 2: *684–9).
  Doctrine: the Sacraments in general and Baptism (with three canons on the reforms relating to the sacraments)
  Reform: Ecclesiastical benefices

THIRTEENTH SESSION (11 October 1551) (Tanner, *Decrees* 2: *693–*702).
  Doctrine: the Eucharist
  Reform: Rights and Duties of Bishops

FOURTEENTH SESSION (25 November 1551) (Tanner, *Decrees* 2: *703–18).
  Doctrine: Sacraments of Penance and Extreme Unction
  Reform: Relations between Bishops and Priests

TWENTY-FIRST SESSION (16 July 1562) (Tanner, *Decrees* 2: *723–32).
  Doctrine: Communion under Both Species
  Reform: Disciplinary measures regarding Priests and their means of subsistence

TWENTY-SECOND SESSION (17 September 1562) (Tanner, *Decrees* 2: *732–41).
    Doctrine: the Sacrifice of the Mass (with a Decree on Abuses to be avoided in celebrating Mass)
    Reform: the Priestly Life and Dispensations

TWENTY-THIRD SESSION (15 July 1563) (Tanner, *Decrees* 2: *742–53).
    Doctrine: the Sacrament of Holy Orders
    Reform: the Call to Holy Orders by the Bishop and the establishment of seminaries

TWENTY-FOURTH SESSION (11 November 1563) (Tanner, *Decrees* 2: *753–74).
    Doctrine: the Sacrament of Matrimony, with canons concerning reforms about marriage
    Reform: Provincial and Diocesan Synods; Pastoral Visitations; Preaching; Cathedral Chapters; Vacancies of episcopal Sees

TWENTY-FIFTH SESSION (3 December 1563) (Tanner, *Decrees* 2: *774–99).
    Doctrine: Purgatory; Devotion to Saints and use of Images
    Reform: Religious Orders and Monks; a Decree of "General Reform" consisting of twenty-one chapters dealing with very diverse issues, aimed at complementing all the preceding decrees

The sketch above makes it clear that the council was not able to achieve a completely consistent parallel in its discussions and resolutions about any given issue of doctrine and reform. This is not surprising when one considers the turbulent, not to say chaotic, history of a council that was in session during less than six of its eighteen years and that the bishops and theologians at its closing sessions were not the same persons who were there at its opening. Nevertheless, on strategic, traditional points of doctrine, such as Sacred Scripture, the Eucharist, and Holy Orders, the council was not content merely to repeat and clarify those doctrines. It was moved by a clear intention to suppress abuses in their regard and to implement pastoral initiatives and other practical steps to be taken in doing so.

The council Fathers remained divided, however, on several issues. The most delicate of these concerned the nature of the episcopacy. The council's theological discussions, proposals, and compromises about whether bishops were consecrated by divine right were muddied by the disciplinary problem of the bishops' obligation to reside in their dioceses. Issues like that allow us to see the complexity of what was at stake when doctrine and discipline were so closely connected and when decisions about them had weighty consequences about how papal primacy and ecclesiology in general were to be understood.

The Divine Right of the Episcopacy

The Council of Trent never set out to construct an explicit ecclesiology, nor could it have done so. Its discussions reveal so many hesitations and differences, not to say contradictions, about certain relevant issues that it would have been impossible – both politically and theologically – to come to agreement. Nevertheless the council Fathers could and did enunciate a clear doctrine of the sacrament of Holy Orders, because they could all agree that the denial of the ministerial priesthood in favour of the priesthood of the faithful common to all baptized Christians was one of the most decisive differences between Catholicism and the Protestant Reformers.

From May 1547 the Council of Trent began to examine many of the errors of Protestants in respect to the sacrament of Holy Orders. Theologians and council Fathers worked together to draw up texts that they submitted to a definitive vote of the delegates. Canon 4 denied that bishops chosen by the people – not by the pope – were consecrated by divine right. It further ruled that, by divine right, bishops had the power to ordain priests. These texts directly refuted Protestant views on Holy Orders. Due to the opposition of the emperor, however, they were not put to a vote in September 1547, as had been planned. As events later proved, this delay permitted the Council to refine and improve its reflections on this essential issue. In the early discussions, its conception of the episcopacy was still too purely concerned with "jurisdictional authority." By putting the accent too heavily on the bishops' governing authority, it had detached the episcopacy in some ways from the sacrament of Holy Orders of which, at that time, the priesthood (presbyterate) was thought to be the measure and the plenitude.[3]

The council had many times invoked the divine right status of the office of bishop in relation to residence of bishops in their dioceses. This had figured among the topics of discussion about the disciplinary decree of the sixth session, but it did not figure in the text that was finally voted upon and approved.[4]

The discussions on Holy Orders emerged again during the second phase of the Council. This time the theologians put the accent clearly on the divine institution of the episcopacy. The text they drew up states that "Bishops have been instituted by divine right as superior to priests." For the majority of the Fathers, however, this affirmation was more concerned with a hierarchical order than with the nature of the sacrament of Holy Orders. The doctrine and the canons were ready to be voted upon at the end of January 1552, but the arrival of delegations of Protestants at that time caused the vote to be postponed. The presence of the Protestants also caused enough of a stir among certain delegates that it was one of the factors for which the council was suspended. Meeting In Bologna, the Curial delegation then brought forth its view on bishops. It declared that the authority of bishops did come from God, but this was only indirectly. It was the pope who directly conferred their authority.[5] Once again, however, the discussion was not followed up. No one, however, could be unaware that the stakes were high. The decision on a decree about the relations between the pope and the bishops would become so crucial during the third phase of the council that, as Hubert Jedin has said, it stirred up a veritable crisis.

The objective of the papal legates in that third phase (1562–1563) was to establish the conjoint doctrinal and disciplinary program that the council had agreed to achieve. They therefore sought to avoid divisive debates. Just as the French bishops with their Gallican ten-

---

3   Jean Bernhard et al., *L'Époque de la Réforme et du concile de Trente* (Paris, 1989), 186.
4   Joseph Lecler, SJ, et al., *Trente* (Paris, 1981), 149.
5   *CT* 6.1: 395.

dencies agreed to avoid all mention – pro or con – of the superiority of councils over the pope, so did the Augustinian superior general Girolamo Seripando propose that all mention of the divine right of bishops be avoided, leaving the question open.

But the delegates who favoured a strengthening of the episcopate would have no part of that. Led by the bishop of Granada, Pedro Guerrero, who was acting on the advice of his theologian, Pedro de Fonseca, they continued to call for a reopening of the discussion.[6] The debates therefore continued, taking up most of the council's time during the month of October. It was at this point that the superior general of the Jesuits, Diego Laínez, proposed using a distinction between the power of Holy Orders and the power of jurisdiction. Both, he said, were bestowed by God for the purpose of saving souls, but they were not bestowed in the same way. The first came directly from God by sacramental ordination, the second came indirectly by commission through the pope. But could one, in this second case, really speak of divine right? According to Laínez, one could do so, if one made the following distinction: considered in itself and as a whole, the jurisdictional power of bishops was of divine right, like that of the bishop of Rome; but, because of the mediation of the pope, this could not be said of each individual bishop. Laínez' position was close to that of the curialists, but it in no way convinced those who favoured the divine right of bishops purely and simply. In the vote taken on 20 October 1562, however, these latter suffered a setback, since they could only amass fifty-three votes against one hundred and one. They still refused to admit defeat, and they received support when the French bishops, led by the Cardinal of Lorraine, arrived in mid-November. For them, the divine right of bishops was "clearer than the light of day."[7]

6 *CT* 9: 34.
7 Alain Tallon, *La France et le concile de Trente (1518–1563)* (Rome, 1997), 346. For the full scope of Laínez's thought on this matter, see Hartmann Grisar, SJ, ed., *Jacobi Laínez Disputationes tridentinae: Ad manuscriptorum fidem edidit et commentariis historicis instruxit*, vol. 1: *Disputatio de origine jurisdictionis episcoporum et de romani pontificis primatu* (Innsbruck; Regensburg, 1886).

The debate had already resumed in early November because of the thorny disciplinary question of whether bishops were obliged to reside in their dioceses. Put simply, if the obligation were *de jure divino*, belonging by divine right to the episcopal office itself, no one could dispense from it, as popes were in the habit of doing. The stakes were indeed high, and so the debates continued on this juridical point between delegates proposing a "pontifical" ecclesiology and those favouring an "episcopal" one.

In the end, the legates side-stepped the question by looking at it from a purely disciplinary fashion – just as the proposed decree in the sixth session in 1547 had done. But here they found themselves in a situation where disciplinary reform implicitly reflected upon dogma. For, if one could admit the legitimacy of dispensations from the obligation of residing, then this could not be of divine right but only of human jurisdiction. This was a clear signal to the delegates that employing the concept of "divine right" equally to both the episcopacy itself and to the residence of bishops led to an impasse. Still, a resolution was reached only after four more months of sometimes unruly debate, of postponing decisive voting, and especially by weeks of negotiations by the new papal legate, Giovanni Morone, with the French bishops. He came up with a final wording of the text which withheld condemning either opinion yet implied no reduction in the authority of the Holy See.[8]

Chapter IV of the decree issued by the twenty-third session of the Council declared that, as the Apostle[9] says, bishops "have been made by the Holy Spirit to rule the Church of God."[10] This formula gave pride of place to apostolic succession but, as proposed by the Cardinal of Lorraine, left open to interpretation the meaning of "to rule" (*regere*) while still managing to include jurisdiction in the sacramental power of the episcopacy. Canon 8 of the decree simply mentioned "the bishops who are elevated by the authority of the pope,"[11] without entering into a definition of papal primacy.

8   Lecler et al., *Trente*, 383.
9   Not Paul but Acts 20:28.
10 *CT* 9: 621. See Tanner, *Decrees* 2: *743, lines 11–12.
11 Tanner, *Decrees* 2: *744.

As for the issue of the "rulers of the churches" (*rectores ecclesi-arum*) residing in their dioceses, the very first canon of the decree of reform recalls the reasons which, within certain limits, impose it and declare it to be obligatory for all, even for cardinals. But, despite the stringent terms of the canon, its force was lessened by the initial use of "divine precept" (*cum praecepto divino*), a formula that was vague enough not to call into play all the consequences that the two sides, holding opposite views on residence (and thus on plurality of benefices), either wished or feared.[12]

This example makes it clear that the Council of Trent, limiting itself to refuting the errors of the Reformers and to providing the means of a true reform, did not consider it necessary to construct an exhaustive theology of the Church. That would be the task of Vatican I and of Vatican II, both of which would reaffirm the sacramental character of the episcopate – something that was never more than a minority opinion at Trent. The model of the Church constructed at Trent was to be affirmed and elaborated upon by theologians of the late sixteenth and seventeenth centuries. But their work would have been impossible and meaningless without the living reality of the Church that rested on the apparatus and the structures given it by the council.

12 Tallon, *La France et le concile de Trente*, 792. See Tanner, *Decrees* 2: *744, line 24.

CHAPTER EIGHT

The Apparatus of Reform

The Council of Trent alone could not have set up all the different instruments, tools, or provisions that it might have thought necessary to implement and consolidate the Catholic Reformation. Only certain ones, such as new editions of Sacred Scripture, had been foreseen and specifically recommended by its reform decrees. Others, such as the Index of Prohibited Books and the catechism, had been worked on in a preliminary way by the council Fathers themselves, but had not been advanced very far. This is why, in a decree voted at the closure of the council on 4 December 1563, provision was made to entrust the sovereign pontiff with the task of preparing and publishing the Index of books, the catechism, the breviary, and the missal.

These were some of the tools that the artisans of reform of the Catholic Church would use for nearly four centuries. They would take on real importance in the measure that they put into practice the spirit of the conciliar documents while adapting them to everyday demands. This was especially true for the catechism. Certain other "instruments" were more directly ordered towards diffusing and making known the council's doctrines, while still others served in the public or private celebration of the Church's liturgical actions.

The Protestant Reformers had used biblical texts to protest and denounce what they considered to be doctrinal errors in the Church. Like humanists before them they had attached great importance to assuring that the texts in use were truly the authentic, original ones. The Roman Church had shared that concern just as early, although it would take several decades for the Church to achieve the goal.

Editions of Sacred Scripture

Some of the council Fathers had called for a new edition of the Septuagint – the Greek version of the Jewish Scriptures.[1] That task

---

1   The Septuagint had its origin for the most part in Alexandria, Egypt, probably between 300 and 150 BC. It included some books not found in the Hebrew scrip-

was entrusted to a commission appointed by Cardinal Felice Peretti Montalto, the future Pope Sixtus V, and headed by Cardinal Antonio Carafa. It was published in 1587 and completed the next year by a second volume containing the literal Latin version.[2]

The council had declared the Latin Vulgate Bible to be "authentic" and "to be maintained" in the Roman Church. It was thought to be sufficiently close to the oldest manuscripts to serve the purposes of teaching and of settling controversy. Still, the council mandated the preparation of a "critical" edition – that is, one based on the best manuscripts, showing variants between them. Pope Sixtus V named another commission for this task, and he once again showed confidence in Antonio Carafa by appointing him its head. The Jesuit scholar Robert Bellarmine was one of its members. Sixtus was impatient with its progress, since he thought the commission was attaching undue importance to too many textual variants. Despite his age[3] and his busy agenda, Sixtus therefore took the task in hand himself, intervening directly and without sufficient expertise in determining the final text. This "Sixtine" edition of the Vulgate, finished and printed in May 1590, thus met with a lot of polite criticism from Catholic scholars and with mockery from Protestant ones. When the pope died three months later, in August 1590, it was immediately withdrawn from sale, and attempts were made to buy back all the copies that had been distributed *gratis*. This was, of course, impossible, and the failed attempt became the target of sneering aspersions from certain Protestant authors.

Urged by Robert Bellarmine, popes Gregory XIV and then Clement VIII ordered a scientific revision of the text to be finalized. By incorporating and improving the work done by the Carafa commission, it was finally promulgated on 9 November 1592. Known as the "Sixto-

---

tures. These latter were incorporated into the Latin Vulgate Bible as canonical, but they constitute what other Bible versions term "Apocrypha." Found in many manuscripts, the Septuagint was printed for the first time in the Complutensian Bible of Cardinal Francisco Ximénes de Cisneros (see above, p. 51).

2   Giancarlo Pani, "Un centenaire à rappeler: l'édition sixtine de la Septante," in *Théorie et pratique de l'exégèse*, ed. Irena Backus and Francis Higman (Geneva, 1990), 413–28.

3   He was sixty-four when elected pope in 1585 and sixty-eight when he died.

Clementine Vulgate," it remained authoritative in the Roman Church until the appearance of the new critical edition undertaken at the beginning of the twentieth century.[4] Because the use of biblical translations into modern languages was forbidden, this Latin Vulgate edition was used exclusively in the Catholic liturgy and para-liturgical devotions. It impregnated a certain stamp – Paul Claudel called it a Catholic "manner" – that has been strongly admired and defended by many.

The Profession of Faith

The so-called "Profession of Faith of the Council of Trent" is in fact one that Pope Pius IV promulgated on 13 November 1564, nearly a year after the council had ended. In its final sessions, the council had recommended that a modern creed incorporating the Catholic dogmas not mentioned in the ancient creeds, such as the number of sacraments as seven, Eucharistic transubstantiation, devotion to the Virgin Mary and the saints, Roman primacy, etc. Such an initiative can be seen as a Catholic response to the growing number of Protestant "confessions of faith," beginning with the one presented by the Lutherans at the Diet of Augsburg in 1530. It seemed logical that Catholics, too, should have a simple and inclusive formulation of the dogmas professed in the Roman Church.

Actually, the "Catechism of the Council"[5] that grew to have great import was originally intended for the use of pastors. Its wide diffusion, many translations, and adaptations did, in fact, give it a prominent role in Catholic preaching of the Gospel both in Europe and in missionary fields.

The Roman Catechism

Very early, the council Fathers had planned the publication of a catechism "based on Sacred Scripture and the orthodox Fathers of the

4   Undertaken under the orders of Pope Pius X in 1907, only the Old Testament was completed. It was used in the *Biblia Sacra Vulgata* (Stuttgart, 1969; 5th ed. 2007). The Second Vatican Council commissioned the *Nova vulgata Bibliorum sacrorum editio* (Rome, 1979).

5   For an English translation see *Catechism of the Council of Trent for Parish Priests, issued by Order of Pope Pius V*, ed. and trans. John A. McHugh, OP, and Charles J. Callan, OP (New York; London, 1923; many reprints).

Church."[6] When some of its delegates were gathered in Bologna in 1547, they reflected more closely on what they should produce. They determined it should be a resolutely Catholic exposition of the faith, based on good pedagogical method, intended especially for priests, and stamped with an official status.

It was only during the third period of the council, however, that the Bolognese reflections were finally taken up. As we have seen, other Catholic catechisms already existed. Some of the bishops proposed adopting the one composed by Peter Canisius,[7] but Canisius himself urged that a different text be composed that would reflect council decisions and carry the stamp of its authority. In January 1562, the papal legates were busy trying to produce such a text. It was only seriously taken in hand after reception of the *Libellus reformationis* (May 1562) of Emperor Ferdinand, which formally called for the elaboration of a Summary of Christian doctrine.[8] The French delegation joined in the same demand after they arrived in 1563. Completion of a catechism had thus become a matter of political concern.

Thus, with the council still in session, the Fathers began by parcelling out the various tasks in the traditional order: the *Credo* (assigned to the Spanish), the Ten Commandments, the "Our Father," and the sacraments. In October a more formal commission was set up. The archbishop of Zara (Dalmatia), Muzio Calini, was delegated to liaise with a new group that would be constituted after the council. Formation of that group was left to Charles Borromeo, a nephew of Pius IV. He turned the preparation of the catechism over to theologians who had both his trust and that of the archbishop of Braga (Bartolomeu Fernandez, later known as "a Martyribus"), who had a remarkable impact on the reform movement at the council.

Although the work on the catechism advanced rather quickly at first, its publication was delayed because some commission members believed that materials from Bartolomé de Carranza's *Commen-*

---

6   *CT* 5: 73.
7   See above, p. 57.
8   *CT* 13.1: 678. Impatient with what he considered to be a ponderous pace in dealing with disciplinary matters, Ferdinand also proposed a number of specific reforms in head and members.

taries,[9] which they considered to be heretical, had made their way into the catechism. In order to avoid all such contentions, a new commission was charged with revising the text. The Dominican Leonardo Marini (1509–1573) played an essential role in most stages of this final work. The publication of the Latin text[10] took place in October 1566, and was soon followed by vernacular versions in German, Polish, French, and Castilian Spanish.

The Preface to this "Catechism of the Council of Trent" (also known as the "Roman" catechism) explains that its three principal components – the doctrines of faith, Sacred Scripture, and preaching – were deliberately chosen, first, to refute the "false prophets" and, second, to provide Christians with everything they needed to know about the Catholic faith. The members knew full well that success in these two goals would depend on their catechism being understood and used by parish priests, who were charged with instructing the people. That, in turn, depended on four essential conditions (they called them "pillars"): first, those using the catechism must freely accept the doctrines of faith; second, they must live a Christian life with the help of the sacraments; third, they must be guided by a Gospel-oriented interpretation of the Ten Commandments; and, fourth, their lives must be nourished by the different forms of prayer contained in the "Our Father." This catechism, when effectively preached, with its roots firmly planted in Scripture and its solid theological framework, was to become one of the most effective instruments of reform to emerge from the council.

The Index of Prohibited Books

With the Index of Prohibited Books the post-conciliar Church went on the offensive, although the Index figured very little in the daily life of most Christian people. The universities of Paris and Lou-

9 *Commentarios ... sobre el catechismo cristiano* (Antwerp, 1558). This incident intensified the differences between Rome and Spain. See also above, pp. 57–8.
10 *Catechismus ex decreto Concilii Tridentini, ad parochos, Pii Quinti Pont. Max. iussu editus* (Rome, 1582). See the modern critical edition, *Catechismus romanus*, ed. Pedro Rodriguez and Ildefonso Adeva (Rome; Navarra, 1989).

vain had been the first to issue catalogues of forbidden books.[11] The first Roman Index[12] was published by Pope Paul IV in 1557. It cast too wide a net, condemning indiscriminately all books published anonymously since 1519, because that was one of the ways for Protestant propaganda to be circulated. It condemned the complete works of a number of authors, even though only one or two of their works had been censured for cause. Pius IV therefore ordered the council to prepare a new edition of the Index and to explain the criteria on which the books listed in it were condemned. Not being able to get far with this task, the council entrusted its accomplishment to the pope himself.

The new Index[13] was promulgated on 24 March 1564. As required, its Preface carefully explained the criteria for each category of the books listed. Category Two contained the works of Luther, Zwingli, Calvin, and other Protestant authors, and all other books officially condemned since 1515. Another category included a certain number of Bibles, especially vernacular translations, which were considered to contain errors or to favour Protestantism. Rule 4 of the Preface laid out the complex and daunting procedures required to obtain permission to read even an approved translation of the Bible. One had, first, to get the permission of the parish priest or confessor and then of the bishop. (This process later became even more difficult.) Rule 8 explained how the condemnation of some books applied only until specific passages in them were corrected. Immoral books and those suspected of magic or necromancy were, of course, also forbidden. In 1571 a Congregation was set up to organize and bring up to date the list of titles of books to be added or dropped from the Index, which was to appear in numerous updated editions until 1967.

11 Paris in 1544, Louvain in 1547. See *Index des livres interdits,* ed. J.M. De Bujanda et al. (Sherbrooke, Québec; Geneva, 1984–2002), vols. 1 and 2.
12 *Index des livres interdits,* ed. J.M. De Bujanda et al., vol. 8: *Index de Rome, 1557, 1559, 1564: Les premiers index romains et l'index du Concile de Trente* (Sherbrooke, Québec; Geneva, 1990).
13 Ibid. For subsequent Roman indexes, see *Index des livres interdits,* ed. J.M. De Bujanda et al., vol. 9: *Index de Rome, 1590, 1593, 1596, avec étude des index de Parme (1580) et Munich (1582)* (Sherbrooke, Québec; Geneva, 1994).

The Missal and the Breviary

A decree issued on 17 September 1562 was directed at abuses in the celebration of the Eucharist. It called for a liturgical reform – although it did not use that modern term. The experts who had worked on the catechism and on the breviary were named as members of this commission. The person charged with directing this work was a famous scholar, Cardinal Guglielmo Sirleto (1514–1585).

The product of their work was promulgated by Pope Pius V on 14 July 1570. It bore the title *Ordo missae*, the name by which it is still known today. This new missal was largely based on the way the proper celebration of the Eucharistic liturgy had been carried out for centuries and which had been attested by the missal approved by the Roman Curia in 1474.[14] It contained certain changes in rubric, i.e. directives about the proper performance of liturgical actions, such as the elevation of the host and the chalice after the consecration of each species. This helped to reinforce the Eucharistic theology that had been emphasized by the council. The desire to unify and simplify pre-existing rites is clearly stated in the Preface. The only ones to be allowed were those that could show an approved usage dating from two centuries earlier, such as the rites of Milan (Ambrosian) and of Lyons, the Dominican rite, the Carthusian rite, and other particular rites. The council's liturgists had opted for a simple, subdued celebration of the Mass – in contrast to the more elaborate liturgies of the Eastern Church. The numbers of prefaces, sequences, and Scripture readings for saints' feasts were reduced, making it possible for the priest and even some of the faithful to commit the liturgy to memory. Great stress was placed on exact observance of the rubrics in order to correct many deplorable abuses and to help attain the goal of a unified liturgy that would give witness to a unified Catholicity.

The recitation of the breviary was an integral part of the Tridentine reformation of priestly life. It aimed at eliminating two excessive tendencies that had been introduced earlier: first, the many doubtful legends that had crept into the breviary over the centuries, especially

14 See Joseph H. Jungmann, *The Mass of the Roman Rite: Its Origins and Development (Missarum sollemnia)*, trans. Francis A. Brunner (New York, 1951–1953; repr. Westminster, Md., 1986), 127–41.

those recounting the lives of saints; and, second, certain neo-pagan classical texts that had been introduced by humanist clerics. The reformed breviary that the former Franciscan guardian general, Francisco Quiñones, had introduced in 1535 had been widely criticized for its bold rejection of many traditional usages and for its accent on the didactic aspect of liturgy. The council decided to opt for a middle way between the provocative innovations of Quiñones and the excessive length and doubtful legends of the traditional breviary.

The commission that was named for this task included, once again, Sirleto, Marini, and several other scholars who had helped prepare the new catechism and the missal. The new breviary was promulgated on 9 July 1568 by Pius V. Traditional devotions such as the Office of the Blessed Virgin Mary and the Office of the Dead were given due importance, so that the breviary could claim to be not a new breviary but a "reformed" one. Once again, deliberate choices were made for a unification of the liturgy, so that the one Church, no matter where it found itself, could offer to the one God the homage of one same prayer (*uni Deo unica formula*).

The creation of the Congregation of Rites, combined with the designation of Latin as the sole liturgical language and the decision to permit only texts that conformed to prototypes, all combined to make the public and private prayers of the Roman Church a remarkable force for unity. These measures would inevitably prove problematic in missionary lands. But, in contrast to the diversity found in the different Protestant confessions in Europe, this stress on unity promoted one set of doctrines and one vision of Christianity that assimilated Catholicism and *Romanitas*. Other new structures for the Church would assure that this assimilation would live on.

CHAPTER NINE

The Structures of Reform

The Tridentine Church restored and revivified certain institutions and procedures, such as synods and pastoral visitations, which had been little used or misused at the end of the Middle Ages. But it also set up, within its central government and at the local level, new structures aimed at improving pastoral care in the Church. Thus, as we study the important connections that the Council of Trent established between doctrine and disciplinary reform – a development that we have called the key to Catholic renewal in the sixteenth century – we must not overlook its invisible, yet concrete, ecclesiastical and sacramental structure.

Structures at the Centre

For Catholics the central structure of the Church in Rome governs the Church and implements new decisions affecting it. The pontificate of Sixtus V, in fact, had the weighty task of putting in place a new Curial organization that was destined to function for centuries. True, the Church had already seen many changes and developments required to administer the Papal States and to assure its functioning in Christendom, but the Tridentine reformation obliged Rome to instigate a much more complete restructuring. Much of this happened in one fell swoop twenty-five years after the council, when Pope Sixtus V promulgated the bull *Immensa aeterni Dei* (22 January 1588). As the text of this bull was read, describing, one-by-one, a whole new congeries of Roman congregations to be continued or established, it cannot have failed to impress on his audience that they were hearing a new ecclesiastical constitution designed to implement a radical reform *in capite* of the Church.

At the head of all the structures was the pre-existing Congregation of the Holy Inquisition, called the "Holy Office." It had been created by Pope Paul III in 1542 as a court of appeal in heresy trials, and Paul IV had strengthened its role. It was now empowered to deal with all "matters of faith," a term which, as we have seen, characterized the priority of dogma as the foundation on which the visible Church is built. Its place at the top level of government under the pope determined its role as tribunal of last resort in matters of heresy, schism, the practice of magic, and abuses in administering the sacraments. With the exception of certain privileged courts of inquisition, such as the one for Spain and its empire, the jurisdiction of the Holy Office extended (in theory) to all Catholic areas and all members of the Church. In practice, its jurisdiction was always strongest in Italy. Some historians believe its creation in 1542 and its strengthening in 1588 to have been the most important development in the reform of Catholicism.

The Congregation of the Apostolic Signature, known also as the "Signature of Grace," was charged with handling pardons that fell outside the scope of ordinary tribunals. Because that function often overlapped with those of other Church bodies, it would be assumed in the seventeenth century by the Apostolic Datary, which handled requests not concerned with benefices. As we saw in Chapter Four,[1] the *Consilium* in 1537 had called for its reform.

The Congregation of the Consistory was created to prepare the consistories, the meetings of cardinals whose function was to recommend the creation of new cardinals, the nomination of bishops, the delegation of legates, and the territorial boundaries of dioceses. With the pope as its president, this Congregation assumed a role of gathering information and of reflection on major issues of government.

The Congregation of Rites handled liturgical matters, such as modifications to the *Rituale*, the *Ceremoniale*, or the *Pontificale*, and composed liturgical texts to celebrate feasts of newly beatified persons or newly canonized saints.

The Congregation of the Index had the responsibility of watching for the appearance of new books which, in accordance with the rules prescribed by the Council of Trent, should be added to the Index of Prohibited Books. This one, single, and central organism had the advantage of being able to coordinate and consolidate the censures decided by the faculties of theology of various universities. Indeed,

---

1   See above, pp. 41–6.

most of those faculties and universities relinquished issuing their own Indexes in favour of the one issued by the Congregation of the Index.

The Congregation of the Council was charged with interpreting the disciplinary decrees decided at Trent, while the pope reserved to himself decisions about the dogmatic texts. The terms of the bull *Immensa aeterni Dei* that dealt with this Congregation were so wide, however, that they allowed it a certain general oversight of the Catholic reform and a particular jurisdiction over texts emanating from provincial synods.

The Congregation for Religious, which was set up by Sixtus V in 1586, had to see that all the religious orders, including the military orders and the Hospitallers, adhered to the prescriptions legislated for them by Trent. It also had the duty to oversee the rule of cloister of nuns which the council had taken care to ensure would be enforced.

The bull continued the Congregation for Bishops which Pope Gregory XIII had instituted in 1576 to oversee matters concerning the Church hierarchy and apostolic visitations of bishops in their dioceses.

To these eight congregations for general government in the Church the bull *Immensa aeterni Dei* added seven others to handle the administration of the Papal States (its navy, civil affairs, the Roman university, etc.). Sixtus V therefore organized and planned the government of the Church to be extremely pragmatic by incorporating already existing organisms, while modifying their duties, and creating others to carry out other duties necessary to the reform. There can be no doubt, however, that matters concerning the central structure of the Church all rested principally with the Holy Office, the Index, and the Congregation of the Council. They would be joined in 1622 by the Congregation for the Missions, also known as the *Propaganda fide*, of which we will see more later.[2]

It was necessary as well to establish agencies to serve as liaison between the central government and national, diocesan, or local churches. Apostolic nunciatures and *ad limina* visits of bishops to Rome assured these functions.

Already in use as early as the Gregorian reform (eleventh century), the function of nuncio was to become permanent and more

2   See below, p. 128.

important. It had already undergone an evolution in the early sixteenth century. The post-Tridentine Church was now going to use it in a more general capacity for transmitting directives from Rome out to local Church entities. Gregory XIII (1566–1572) established permanent nunciatures to different Italian states, the Empire, France, Spain, and Germany. Towards the end of his pontificate he also dispatched them to regions of mixed confessional allegiance. When the Swiss Catholic cantons wanted to request appointment of a nuncio to set up pastoral visitations, they asked Charles Borromeo to represent their cause in Rome. Giovanni Francesco Bonhomini was sent as nuncio to them in 1579 before being sent on a similar mission, beginning in 1585, to Germany. From that time on Rome had three permanent nunciatures at Cologne, Vienna, and Graz.

Nuncios at that time were not simply ambassadors in contact solely with the governments to which they were accredited. They were also endowed with extensive ecclesiastical functions in the territories where they resided. They conducted diocesan visitations, dealt with pardons and dispensations, kept watch over religious orders – in brief, they oversaw the implementation of the Catholic Reformation. Nuncios were consecrated bishops, and were important personages who had in their service at this time a veritable diplomatic corps maintained by the Holy See and staffed for the most part by men trained in law.

Visits by the various bishops to Rome, *ad limina apostolorum,* served the Church in a complementary way. In his bull *Romanus pontifex* of 20 December 1585, Sixtus V took care to stress the antiquity of this practice. The traditional visits of the successors of the apostles to the tombs of Peter and Paul reinforced the ties of their churches with the see which was entrusted with "a solicitude for all the Churches" – echoing the expression of Saint Paul[3] and used in the most ancient texts affirming the primacy of Rome. Sixtus fixed the timing of these episcopal visits, ranging from every three years for Italian bishops and others residing nearby to every ten years for those residing far away. On each occasion of his *ad limina* visit the bishop was expected to provide

3   2 Cor. 11:28.

the Roman Curia with a detailed report about the life of his local Church and, of course, about progress made in its reform.

Local Structures

Because disciplinary and moral reforms were intended to take place at local levels, the council tried to inject new life into old ecclesiastical structures at those levels and to create new ones as well. The gathering together of local church assemblies, called councils or synods, was one such ancient practice. In its Session 23 (11 November 1563), Canon II of the "Decree on Reform," the Council of Trent had cited their usefulness and their necessity.[4]

Convened normally every year at the diocesan level and every three years at the archdiocesan, or provincial, one, the synod was the principal occasion where the mandates and recommendations of the conciliar decrees were received and implemented and where they could be adapted to the practical needs of the local Church. Synodal documents, printed and circulated, had to be approved by the Congregation of the Council. In addition to requests made to Rome, synodal reports contain details about the decisions and actions taken against sometimes astonishing and picturesque abuses. As such they often furnish historians with a rich and detailed panorama of Christian life and of matters requiring reform at that time – as indeed do the reports brought to Rome by bishops making their canonical visits. By mandating both synods and *ad limina* visits, the council provided important and practical means to implement necessary reforms and to exercise control from the centre over parishes scattered all over Europe.

Probably the best example of synodal activity is that of the six provincial councils presided over by Charles Borromeo in Milan from 1565 to 1579. They provide a paradigm of what a synod was designed to do. The synods made sure that preachers knew the basic tenets of the faith and helped them to adapt their sermons to the needs of the faithful. Preachers were shown how to pray and how to help the

---

4   Tanner, *Decrees* 2: *761.

people to pray. Borromeo's *Acta ecclesiae Mediolanensis*[5] describe the pastoral administration of the sacraments – especially the Eucharist and confession of sins – and deal with proper catechetical instruction. They record the foundation and progress of a seminary for the proper formation of priests. Borromeo's *Acta* circulated widely and thus served as a model to other dioceses of how synods could implement Catholic reform in a given place.

In its twenty-third session on 15 July 1563, the Council of Trent had created its most celebrated local institution – seminaries to form future priests. Building on earlier initiatives, the council had in effect given a permanent structure capable of providing young aspirants to the priesthood a way of life that the universities could not provide, even if their colleges followed an approved model. Priority was to be given to poor students. As an integral part of the diocesan structure, seminaries were to receive the full attention of the bishops. The word "seminary," as employed in the decree of reform,[6] was purposely chosen as an allegory: the "seed" of priestly vocations was to be carefully nourished by seminary directors, just as plants sown in a garden.

Some leading reforming bishops made it a point of honour to establish separate houses of formation, known as "minor seminaries," for very young candidates. Among the first were Charles Borromeo in Milan (1564), Bartolomeu Fernandez (a Martyribus) in Braga (Portugal), and Charles de Guise, Cardinal of Lorraine, at Reims (1567). Some places, such as Spain, took longer to set up seminaries because of financial reasons. In France, the Wars of Religion (1561–1598) prevented rapid establishment and adequate financing in most areas.

In some places, the papal nuncios had to exert pressure on princes and bishops to set up seminaries. This was often the case in the German Empire. The seminary of Eichstätt (Bavaria), however, opened quite early, in 1564. It was entrusted to the Jesuits, who provided a plan of studies based on their experience in forming members of the Society, particularly in the Collegio Romano. Saint Peter Canisius worked hard to get seminaries started in other imperial dioceses.

5   (Milan, 1582).
6   Session 23, Canon 18. See Tanner, *Decrees* 2: *750–3; *Canons and Decrees*, 175–9.

Seminaries for emigrants, for example the ones established at Douai and Reims for young English Catholics, were imbued with an intense missionary vocation to a spiritual reconquest of their land. Their curriculum combined a kind of preparation, even a yearning, for martyrdom for that cause with an intense humanistic education. Seminaries of this kind came under the direct authority of the Congregation for the Propagation of the Faith, which also created its own seminary in Rome, the Collegio Urbano, in 1627.

The general spread of seminaries would effect a profound change not only in the quality but also in the image of the Catholic priest. A deep priestly spirituality developed in the seventeenth century, especially in France.[7] It was not simply the result of putting seminaries in place. That merely gave a locus and a visible structure where the change could take place. What was really behind the deepening of priestly spirituality[8] was the ecclesiology implicit in the doctrine of the Council of Trent – an ecclesiology that produced the invisible structure of the new Catholic priesthood.

The Invisible Structure

The most essential dogmatic achievement of the Council of Trent occurred during all three of its phases, when it engaged in discussions about the theology of the sacraments. The discussions began as a way to counter the attacks on Catholic sacraments by the Protestant Reformers, but that soon changed. The council made a thorough, positive reexamination of the seven sacraments that would forge the invisible structure of the Catholic Reform for the next four centuries.

---

7   In France three new religious orders undertook the formation of priests in seminaries as a special apostolate in the first half of the seventeenth century: the Lazaristes (Vincentians), founded by St Vincent de Paul; the Eudists (Society of Jesus and Mary), founded by St John Eudes; and a pious society of diocesan priests known as Sulpicians (founded by Jean-Jacques Olier).

8   Cardinal Pierre de Bérulle (1575–1629) established in 1611 the Congregation of the Oratory in France on the model of that first founded in Rome by St Philip Neri. He was a leading proponent of the spiritual development of ordained priests and religious men and women. See Stéphane-Marie Morgain, *Pierre de Bérulle et les Carmélites de France* (Paris, 1995).

The very reaffirmation of the number of sacraments at seven was already a significant indication of the council's orientation. The council Fathers were taking only a first, basic step when, in negating the Protestants' retaining only two sacraments, they reaffirmed the Catholic doctrine that all seven are contained in Scripture and that, at least implicitly, Christ instituted each one of them. They made this declaration of the doctrine of seven sacraments on the basis of their close study of the Bible, of apostolic traditions, and of medieval theology. The Fathers were exercising the task and the privilege of the Church of interpreting the Sacred Scriptures.

After approval of the decrees on original sin and justification, the Fathers quite logically next took up their consideration of the sacrament of Baptism, since it is the one which essentially constitutes the Church. Against the Anabaptists they showed that infant baptism is the touchstone of a harmonious and diversified vision of the Church: "If anyone says that children, because they make no act of faith, should not after the reception of baptism be numbered among the faithful, ... let him be anathema."[9]

Turning to the sacrament of the Eucharist, the council declared it to be "the very sacrament which the Saviour left in his Church as a symbol of its unity and love, whereby he wished all Christians to be mutually linked and united."[10] Jesus Christ, the one perfect priest, the unique source of salvation, offered his very self on the altar of the cross. But his death did not end his priesthood. At the last supper, in fact, he instituted an unbloody sacrifice in which the one, bloody sacrifice of the cross is made present to the faithful. The Mass is the Church's response to his command. It is perpetuated until the end of time in the Church, and its power (*virtus*) is applied daily for the remission of sins.[11]

---

9 Session 7 (3 March 1547), "Canons on the Sacrament of Baptism," 13. See Tanner, *Decrees* 2: *686; *Canons and Decrees*, 54.

10 Session 13 (11 October 1551), "Decree on the Most Holy Sacrament of the Eucharist," Introduction. See Tanner, *Decrees* 2: *693, lines 23–5; *Canons and Decrees*, 72.

11 Session 22 (17 September 1562), "Teaching and Canons on the Most Holy Sacrifice of the Mass," ch. 1. See Tanner, *Decrees* 2: *732, lines 3–8; *Canons and Decrees*, 144–5.

Martin Luther was fully conscious of the crucial role of Eucharistic theology in Catholicism when he wrote, "If we can do away with the Mass we will have completely done away with the pope."[12] The council did not directly respond to Luther by giving a definition of the "sacrifice of the Mass." Instead it showed how the sacrificial quality of the Mass is no denial of divine liberty. It is the very foundation of — the essential reason for — the sacramental priesthood in the Church and the very basis for its ministry and authority.

This is why, instead of defining the priesthood by its role of preaching, the Council of Trent looked at the sacrament of Holy Orders as crucial to the very inner working of the sacramental system: Eucharist, Baptism, Penance. It is the power to consecrate, offer, and distribute the Eucharist and the power to remit or retain sins which defines the essence of the visible priesthood of the New Covenant.[13] Conferred by a sacrament, the priesthood confers an indelible character and helps give the Church its hierarchical structure. It therefore legitimizes the distinction between clergy and the laity as something willed by Christ himself.

The council confirmed that the sacrament of Penance originated in the command and authority that Christ gave to his apostles to forgive sins. Its sacramental objectivity, signified by the concept and expression *ex opere operato*, is much more than a purely psychological or spiritual rejuvenation. Rather, it procures for the penitent God's grace of pardon. Thus, like the other sacraments, Penance is founded on the unique sacrifice of Christ on the cross.[14]

No definition of the post-Tridentine Catholic Church could omit the central, defining role of these same seven sacraments that are "perceived by our senses," as Robert Bellarmine says. By affirming the seven sacraments as dogma, the council made clear the coherence of its implicit ecclesiology. The Church draws believers into itself by

12 *Contra Henricum regem Angliae* (1522), WA 10.2: 220, line 13. Not in *LW*.

13 Session 23 (15 July 1563), "Canons on the Sacrament of Order." See Tanner, *Decrees* 2: *743–4; *Canons and Decrees*, 160–1.

14 Session 14 (25 November 1551), "Teaching concerning the Most Holy Sacrament of Penance," contains 9 chapters and 15 canons. See Tanner, *Decrees* 2: *703–9, *711–13; *Canons and Decrees* 88–99, 101–4.

Baptism, but through the Eucharist it also perpetuates itself by the institution of Holy Orders, whose power is assured by Christ himself when he gave his apostles the power to bind and to loose.

Reform of discipline founded on doctrine, or dogma put into practice by reform of discipline: neither of these aspects of post-Tridentine Catholicism could have endured or had any power at all without the personalities who gave life to the Catholic Reformation. They served both as illustrations of it and as examples for others to imitate.

CHAPTER TEN

Some Agents of Reform

Whether by personal conviction or simply acting under obedience, a great number of clerics and lay persons worked over many years to implement the spirit of the Catholic reform that emerged from Trent. It would be a great disservice to ignore their role in giving the reform a secure and lasting place in the life of the Church. In the chapter that follows this one we shall therefore focus our attention on them and their work. In this present one, however, we want first to evoke certain leading personalities who, either by their actions or their publications, had a particularly decisive influence on the way countless Catholics worshipped and worked to reform the Church.

We have chosen five figures whose responses to the call for renewal make them emblematic of all the others. Two of these five – Charles Borromeo, archbishop of Milan, who inaugurated the official work of the Tridentine reform, and Francis de Sales, whose career was flourishing at its closure – were pastors. One, Pius V, was the pope whom we have already seen to be so zealous in setting up ways and means of carrying out the reform. The fourth, Teresa of Avila, embodied the role of feminine religious life and mystical spirituality to become one of the foundational images of the Catholic renewal. Finally, there was Robert Bellarmine, a systematic theologian whose ecclesiology put its stamp on Catholicism for centuries. All five dominated their world; all five have been canonized saints. In each can be seen the amalgam of action and contemplation, of pastoral practice and dogmatic or spiritual theology, which was the driving force of the reform of Catholicism at that time.[1]

---

1   Ignatius of Loyola might well have been included in this list, but the work of his Society of Jesus is represented in other ways in this book. See John W. O'Malley, *The First Jesuits* (Cambridge, Mass., 1993), for the significance of Ignatius and his companions.

Charles Borromeo, or the Exemplar of the Reform

Born in 1538 at Arona on Lake Maggiore in northern Italy, Charles Borromeo received both a clerical and a legal education. His maternal uncle, Pope Pius IV (1559–1565), following the practice of Renaissance popes, was a blatant practitioner of nepotism. He made Charles the cardinal-archbishop of Milan and bestowed on him many other titles and benefices. He appointed him what we today would call Secretary of State. But, although he had been caught up at such an early age in that old system of privileges and dispensations, when Charles accepted ordination he entered into a series of conversions and dedication to a pastoral ideal. In this personal transformation he was like a mirror image of what Catholic reform sought to effect in the whole Church: to instill a soul into an already existing body.

As the "right arm" of his uncle, Charles Borromeo served as liaison between the papacy and the last phase of the Council of Trent. Even though he never personally attended the Council, he was to become the principal artisan and exemplary agent of its decisions. Completely convinced of the crucial importance of the residence of bishops in their dioceses to the council's reform program, he moved from Rome to Milan as soon as he could, and abandoned the trappings of his former life. In an earlier chapter we saw his role in preparing the Roman Catechism. He quickly had it translated into Italian and widely diffused, delegating this task to the Confraternity of Christian Doctrine.

Borromeo attached great importance to the formation of priests and the instruction of the faithful. Following the mandate of the council to create seminaries, he opened in Milan one of the very first ones. To promote the intellectual and spiritual development of the laity he founded colleges and entrusted them to the Jesuits, whose work he greatly admired. He conducted pastoral visitations, travelling from one end of the diocese to the other. His prolific correspondence is a mixture of spiritual direction and political opposition to the ambitions of Spain in the Milanese region. He regularly convened diocesan and provincial synods. Their published proceedings[2] became

2   See above, p. 93.

a model for the Catholic world. His saintly personal life included heroic ministry at the side of the Capuchins during the plague of 1576. The difficulties he encountered, hurdles he jumped, and direct resistance of many enemies of the reforms – extending even to an attempted assassination in 1569[3] – attest to what he was able to accomplish and what he was still trying to accomplish in Milan when he died.

That death came in 1584. At his canonization in 1610 he was proposed as the model of a reforming bishop in the struggle to put the council's reforms into practice. Biographies of his life[4] accented the new image of the ideal shepherd. The same theme is stressed in the iconography that others have used to portray him – for example in the cathedral of Milan, where he is represented in actions of charity.

Pius V, or the Defense of Christianity

At the death of Pope Pius IV in 1565, many persons – among them Charles Borromeo and his circle of reformers – had hoped to elect the brilliant humanist and diplomat Giovanni Morone, who had been the papal legate to the council in its final phase. But, because there had been rumours in 1558 about Morone's orthodoxy and personal life, his supporters could not reach a majority. On 7 January 1566, the choice of the consistory finally settled on an austere Dominican friar, cardinal, and inquisitor, Michele Ghislieri, who chose the name of Pius V. Although he was in some ways the very antithesis of Morone and, as inquisitor, had played a significant role in the 1558 proceedings against Morone, Borromeo soon rallied to him. His accession was a turning point in the papacy; its very image would likewise change with him.

The new pope was born in 1504 to a well-off peasant family. After joining the Dominican Order in 1521, he became a strong advocate of religious poverty and was a critic of the princely life of Renaissance

3   By a disaffected member of the *Umiliati,* a religious order that Borromeo was trying to reform.
4   Two biographies appeared prior to his canonization: that of Agostino Valier (1587) and, more important, that of Carlo Bascapé, bishop of Novara (1592). A third was published at the time of his canonization by the Milanese nobleman and priest Giovanni Pietro Giussano (1610).

popes. His choice as pope was therefore symbolic, and it was confirmed by his actions. "The papacy became an essentially religious power ... . It was a choice for a thinking, praying pope, no longer for one interested only in ruling the Church. It was a choice for a religious power and against a political power; a choice for an escha-tological order and against the realism of the moment."[5] Pius V's papacy, with its decidedly spiritual orientation, set in motion the radical change of focus for the papacy itself at the end of the sixteenth century. His beatification in 1672 and canonization in 1712 can be seen as confirmations of that change.

Recent historians of the Church have tended to treat Pope Saint Pius V as a symbol of traditionalism, but he was much more that that. He was the pope who by his perseverance and labours to interpret the texts and debates of the council – a task he would later turn over to the commission that later became the Congregation of the Council – succeeded in fashioning the instruments of reform[6] which had been planned by the council in its last assemblies, the very sessions he had attended as bishop of Sutri and Nepi with the cardinal's title of "Alessandrino."[7]

Following a tradition long harboured in the fondest hopes of Catholic reformers, Pius V continued the efforts of Paul IV, with whom he had collaborated, to turn his episcopal city Rome into a real model and true centre of Christianity. One of his first steps was to direct bishops who resided in Rome, but who had no function there, to return to their dioceses. He tried to raise the moral standards of Rome, to make it a city renowned for its beauty, morality, and true religion. In a splendid attempt to resurrect Christian Rome and under-cut the neo-paganism of the Roman carnival, he promoted the ancient practice of making pilgrimages to the seven Roman basilicas. It must have been an astonishing sight to see this aged pope trekking along those pilgrimage routes with the whole papal retinue following behind.

---

5   Nicole Lemaître, *Saint Pie V* (Paris, 1994), 330.
6   Named and described in Chapter Nine above.
7   He made a short intervention in the concluding session (26 January 1564) and signed the "Bulla confirmationis concilii." See *CT* 9: 1152, lines 11–12; 9: 1155, line 22.

We should not be surprised, then, to see that the city of Rome was closely associated with what was regarded as a great triumph of Christendom: the defeat of the Turkish fleet in the Gulf of Lepanto on 7 October 1571. The entry into Rome on 4 December of Marcantonio Colonna, the captain of the papal galleys and a citizen of Rome, was consciously staged as a Christianized version of the triumphant entries of conquering armies in ancient times. The feast of Our Lady of the Rosary, which Roman confraternities henceforth celebrated every year on that day, was planned by Pius V and legislated by his successor, Gregory XIII, as a deliberate strategy to make the association of Rome with that victory a permanent symbol in the memory of its citizens.

The battle of Lepanto also had symbolic value as a revival of the "myth of the Crusade."[8] Even though both sides suffered terrible loss of life, never again would the Turks be feared as invincible. It was seen as a sign that if Christendom were once again united in a Holy League under the pope, and if Christians joined fasting to prayer, the infidels could be defeated. Lepanto brought more, however, than just an increase in the prestige of Pius V, the papacy in general, and Rome. It restored a climate of confidence amidst which the reform of Catholicism could be carried out more aggressively and effectively.

On 30 March 1570, Pius V excommunicated Queen Elizabeth of England – an act rendered even more solemn because it had been postponed for years. In Catholic eyes, this action heightened the pope's reputation as defender of the Catholic faith against the Protestants on the Continent and extended it to defender of an even wider Christendom. It made the papacy once again a sign of purity, moral conviction, austerity, and zeal for the reform of the Church that gave it an authentic, spiritual credibility.

Teresa of Avila, or Reform Interiorized

The reform of the Church should obviously be worked out primarily on a spiritual level. Ignatius of Loyola and his companions had

---

8   We borrow this expression from the four-volume thesis (1956) of Alphonse Dupront, published later as *Le mythe de croisade* (Paris, 1997).

understood perfectly what was at stake in this and laboured to bring it about. But the figure of Teresa of Avila, in the context of her native Spanish culture, takes on a particular force in this regard.

The worldly influences from which Teresa fought to save her sisters and the Carmelite Order were not particularly scandalous ones. Rather, they had arisen in the undue influence that the largely aristocratic families of the nuns had on them. The rule of enclosure that the legislation of Trent strongly enforced was contested by those families who, for reasons of household finance, had placed their daughters in the convents. Their parents therefore looked on the convents as an extension of their own households. Teresa recounts how visits and conversations in the parlour of Avila's Convent of the Incarnation were far from edifying.

Having determined quite early that her religious vocation was authentic, Teresa found that the ambiance of apathy and boredom that prevailed around her was a real threat to it. With the help of the young Carmelite friar John of the Cross, Teresa devoted herself to bringing about a reform for the consecrated life of her "daughters." It would be centred on observing the rule of cloister and on the practice of poverty. Her efforts began in 1562 in the Convent of San José and lasted until her death twenty years later. The approach she used was to impart a method of personal and communal prayer which, for the nuns who practiced it, became a doctrine for living a mystical life. This linking of spiritual theology to daily life gave an authentic and lasting basis to her efforts and made her reform of the Carmelite Order one of the turning points of Catholic renewal in the sixteenth century. Saint John of the Cross and Jerome Gracián of the Mother of God were able to effect the same kind of reform on the masculine side of the Carmelites.

At that time in Spain, however, a spirituality oriented towards mysticism was regarded with suspicion of heresy. Counselled by Dominican and Jesuit confessors, however, Teresa was careful to remain completely and manifestly orthodox. She wrote:

> If ever I should say something that is not in conformity with the teaching of the holy Roman Catholic Church, it would be through ignorance and not through malice. That can be held as certain,

and also that through the goodness of God I always am, and will be, and have been subject to her.[9]

Teresa's works became a major resource for Catholic reform. King Philip II, who had met "la Madre" in 1570 and who greatly venerated her, ordered the library at his Escorial Palace to have all of her writings on its shelves. Teresa's secretary and confidante, Ana de San Bartolomé, who had entered the Carmel as a *conversa* and later founded Carmelite convents in France, wrote a *Defensa de la herencia teresiana* which was translated into French, German, Italian, and Flemish. It contributed to the spread of Teresian influence in the Catholic world.

Robert Bellarmine, or the Ecclesiology of Reform

The Jesuit Robert Bellarmine (1542–1621) belonged to the generation whose task was to consolidate the Tridentine reformation. A nephew of Pope Marcellus II, who reigned only twenty-two days (1555), he entered the Jesuit novitiate in 1560 in Rome. After initial studies there, he went for further studies to Padua and then to Louvain, and then entered into a teaching career. In 1576 Pope Gregory XIII called him back to Rome to teach at the Jesuit college and to preach in opposition to heretical doctrine. From 1586 to 1593 he studied closely the works of the Protestant Reformers, and then published his *Disputations concerning the Controversies of the Christian Faith, against the Heretics of these Times*,[10] a book which became a classic of Catholic apologetical literature. In 1598 he published two catechisms, one for adolescents and the other for younger children. They enjoyed great success both in Italy and elsewhere through hundreds of editions and translations, right up to the nineteenth century.

---

9   Prologue to *The Interior Castle*, in *The Collected Works of St Teresa of Avila*, trans. Kieran Kavanaugh, OCD, and Otilio Rodriguez, OCD (Washington, D.C., 1980), 2: 282.

10   See Bellarmine, *Disputationum de controversiis christianae fidei adversus huius temporis haereticos* [*epitome*] (Ingolstadt, 1586–1593; repr. Cologne, 1619–1620; many later editions).

Bellarmine was named a cardinal in 1599 and was consecrated archbishop of Capua in 1602. As one who had long defended the Tridentine directive to bishops to reside in their dioceses, and who had recently complained to Pope Clement VIII about how difficult it was to enforce that norm, he retired to his own remote diocese. There he applied himself vigorously to enforce the reforms of the council. He regularly preached in his cathedral and joined the cathedral canons in their communal prayer of the breviary. But Pope Paul V eventually called him back to Rome and entrusted him with overseeing delicate matters of doctrine. In observance of this duty he was to take part in the first trial of Galileo.

Bellarmine's most important legacy to posterity was his theology of a visible, hierarchical Church which epitomized Tridentine ecclesiology. He wrote in direct opposition to the Protestant position of an invisible, mystical Church. He anchored its visible character not so much in its institutional structure as in its very nature as a community of real persons professing one faith, participating in the same sacraments, and acknowledging the authority of the Roman pontiff. For him, the Church was therefore "as visible as the Venetian Republic."[11] Supported by its own law and acting in its own sphere of competence, the Catholic Church was for Bellarmine a kind of crystallized object. If carried to its ultimate conclusion, his view of the Church accepted and even hardened the growing confessionalization of the Churches. For these reasons, Bellarmine's ecclesiology, especially as it was elaborated by later interpreters, would in the years preceding Vatican II (and in its aftermath) be criticized as too rigid and having too narrow a perspective.

Allied to that ecclesiology was Bellarmine's theory of Church-State relations. Pope Sixtus V had threatened to censure him for not taking a clearly theocratic position about papal power in the secular sphere. Despite that earlier papal threat, Bellarmine reaffirmed in his book *Concerning the Powers of the Supreme Pontiff in Temporal Matters*[12] that the pope had only an indirect power in the temporal

11 Ibid., in "De ecclesia militante," 1: ch. 2, col. 1263.
12 Bellarmine, *De potestate summi pontificis in rebus temporalibus* (Rome, 1610). For an English translation see *Power of the Pope in Temporal Affairs, against William Barclay*, trans. George Albert Moore (Chevy Chase, Md., 1949).

sphere, and that power pertained only in exceptional situations where the spiritual welfare of the people was at stake.

When viewed in all the facets of his actions, books, and personality, Robert Bellarmine is the very embodiment of Tridentine Catholicism: he was a Jesuit, a reforming bishop, a polemicist against Protestants, an author of catechisms and works of piety that knew tremendous success. With his remarkable intelligence and unflagging zeal he was present on all fronts of the reform of Catholicism.

Francis de Sales, or the Reform of Devotion

Even more clearly a product of the second generation of Catholic reformers was Francis de Sales (1567–1622). Scion of a noble family of Savoy, he found himself at the centre of controversy and struggle with the Protestants in Geneva as well as in the kingdom of France itself.

After his early education with the Jesuits in Paris, Francis studied law at Padua in northern Italy, where the pastoral influence of Charles Borromeo was very much alive. After obtaining permission from his father to become a priest, Francis was ordained in 1593 at Annecy, where the bishop of Geneva was living in exile. This ever-present reality inspired him to devote himself to reconverting to Catholicism the region of Chablais which, while formerly under the political aegis of Geneva, had become Calvinist but was a territory of Catholic Savoy. His missionary approach was always irenic and patient, and he was always careful to base his arguments on Sacred Scripture, since his adversaries would accept nothing else. We know from his biographers and also from reports addressed to Pope Clement VIII that on three occasions in 1597 he was able to meet with Théodore de Bèze, Calvin's successor as leader of the Protestant Church in Geneva.

In that same year Francis was named coadjutor bishop of Geneva, and he succeeded to that see in 1602. With his close spiritual friend Jeanne de Chantal, he founded a community of religious sisters. They called the new Order "the Visitation," since they envisioned their nuns visiting the sick and the poor in their homes. But their project ran amiss of the legislation of the Council of Trent that all communities of nuns must be cloistered. The Visitandines were forced to comply.

Francis is an authentic spiritual master. His *Introduction to the* *Devout Life* (1609) was composed in the form of remarks addressed to a spiritual friend, Philothea ("Beloved of God"). In it he invites all Christians – no matter their state of life or their occupation, whether a workman or a woman of society – to practice a life of Christian devotion. He clearly wants to extend the spirit of Catholic reform to all Christian people. By the time of his death there had already been forty editions of this book, numerous translations into other languages, and even an adaptation for use by Protestants.[13] In 1616 he published his *Treatise on the Love of God*, which was based on conferences that he gave to the early Visitandine sisters. In it he tells his imaginary disciple Theotimus ("one who fears God") that he seeks to describe "with childlike simplicity ... the story of the birth, the progress, and the abundance of the operations, properties, advantages, and excellence of divine love." In short, this book is a remarkable treatise of spiritual apologetics.

Although he could never reside in his diocese of Geneva, Francis de Sales took personal charge of the formation of his priests. Between 1606 and 1610, he set up at Annecy an Academy that he called "florimontane" where he urged the teachers to "teach well and teach many things in a short space of time." Renowned as a preacher, even at the court of France, he had no hesitations about personally making pastoral visitations in remote places reached only by risky mountain paths.

By promoting a spirituality ("devotion") accessible to everyone, by his creation of a "devout humanism," by the remarkable equilibrium of duty and kindness that marked his own spiritual life, his governing, and his dealing with controversy, Francis de Sales set an evangelical tone to the reform of Catholicism that made the first years of the seventeenth century one of the high points in the reform movement.

On 12 March 1622, the very year of Bellarmine's death, Pope Gregory XV celebrated the canonization of five persons. This authenticated, so to speak, the importance of the role of personalities in the Catholic Reformation. One of the saints canonized was Isidore the

---

13   See Robert Bireley, *The Refashioning of Catholicism, 1450–1700* (Washington, D.C., 1999), 180.

Farmer, who lived in twelfth-century Madrid. (This was not without significance, because by 1622 Madrid was the capital of a vast Empire of strategic importance to the Church.) The other four were all zealous artisans of Catholic reform. Two of them, Ignatius of Loyola and Francis Xavier, embodied the service to the Church contributed by the Society of Jesus – service in the many forms which were needed at the time, and in particular in missions at Earth's end. The fourth, Teresa of Avila, represented the mystical, contemplative aspect of the reform. The fifth was Philip Neri (1515–1595), who gave a new tone to priestly spirituality by founding the Congregation of the Oratory in Rome in 1564.

Thus, sixty years after the Council of Trent, which had been mainly Mediterranean in its make-up and influence, and twelve years after the canonization of Charles Borromeo, the Church presented to Christendom four Spaniards[14] and one Italian as models of lives that were contemplative, practical, and doctrinal. Their saintliness was also very "Roman." The Society of Jesus was linked in a particular way to the papacy, and Philip Neri exerted his spiritual influence on the clergy and the papal Curia in Rome, where he had lived almost all his life. Since Rome had become the centre of Catholicism, the canonization ceremony was a kind of celebration of Rome itself.

Giovanni Bricci (1579–1645), the author who left us the description of the grandiose canonization ceremony, was himself a citizen of Rome. His detailed description of the pomp and circumstance of the occasion, including a list of the thirty-nine iconographical draperies made for the occasion, shows that it was a deliberately theatrical occasion. Music was played both inside and outside Saint Peter's Basilica which, he said, "by its grandeur, beauty, and architecture surpasses all other churches in the world." Following the blessing of the bull of canonization by the pope, "the people, hearing the sound of trumpets and seized with emotions of great joy and immense jubilation, broke out in applause as a sign of rejoicing and of gratitude towards the saints."[15] The unabashed theatrical side of the reform was

14 Ignatius of Loyola was Basque and Francis Xavier was from the Kingdom of Navarre.
15 Giovanni Bricci, *Relatione sommaria del solenne apparato e cerimonia ... per la canonizatione de gloriosi santi Isidore di Madrid, Ignatio di Loiola, Francesco*

shown again, only twenty years later, when Gian Lorenzo Bernini sculpted his *Ecstasy of Saint Teresa*, placing galleries of onlookers gazing in awe as the saint writhes in mystical rapture.

Should all this be seen to smack of senseless triumphancy or "Counter-Reformation"? No, we can instead discern in such evocative presentations an occasion for popular jubilation. The renewed Catholic Church was holding out to the people examples of the sanctity of men and women who were subject to the same sinful human condition as they themselves but who, through God's grace and their cooperation with it, were able to rise above it. Such manifestations provided a vision of the Church reaching from Earth to Heaven, a moment for the people of God to move beyond a world and a time that was so very new and often so very troubling.

Yes, the reformed Church drew strength from demonstrating that ideals are within human reach. But it could never have taken hold of the minds and hearts of Christians without the contributions of a great corps of agents, of personnel who carried out the widely diversified tasks and assumed the indispensable roles that helped the reform to live on through the centuries.

Xaueria, Teresa di Giesu, e Filippo Nerio Fiorentino ... (Rome, 1622). Bricci is cited by Pietro Tacchi Venturi, "La canonizzazione e la processione dei cinque santi negli scritti e nei disegni di due contemporanei Giovanni Bricci e Paolo Guidotti Borghese," in *La canonizzazione dei Santi Ignazio di Loiola, fondatore della Compagnia di Gesù e Francesco Saverio, apostolo dell'Oriente* (Rome, 1922), 50–72.

CHAPTER ELEVEN

The Personnel of the Reform

The term "personnel" is used here in the way that Jacques Maritain used it: to distinguish the Church as a moral "person" from the Church's "personnel."[1] After the Council of Trent, the Church – the "people of God" and all levels of the hierarchy – gradually and sometimes painfully became imbued with the spirit of a reformed Catholicism. Let us look here at the Church as we would at a fresco – a single image consisting of many parts. There was first of all the papacy: the popes, the cardinals, the Roman curia, and the nuncios – in short what common parlance vaguely and inexactly but suggestively designates under the name "Rome." Then came the episcopacy, the physiognomy of which changed with each nation. One must then see the place reserved for the princes, for they played a decisive role in the make-up of Christendom, and they maintained a firm hold on that role. Then there were the priests, and particularly pastors of parishes, who were the principal mediators between the upper echelons of hierarchy and the people. Next were the members of religious orders, especially those who underwent at this time a remarkable permutation towards apostolic work. They contributed an element of devotedness and generosity singularly apt at providing the social and charitable services that the State expected from established religion. Finally, we must not overlook those who are sometimes called "committed lay persons," who gave the Church its basic framework and made up its fundamental local units.

Rome

Rome as the Babylon of the Apocalypse: this mocking view of Rome by the Protestant Reformers was only part of the reason why the papacy sought to project a better image of the papacy and of

---

1   Jacques Maritain, *On the Church of Christ: The Person of the Church and Her Personnel*, trans. Joseph W. Evans (Notre Dame, Ind., 1973).

Rome. The popes who were interested in reform were conscious of the old truth that an authentic religious reformation cannot take place without a reform at the top (*in capite*). We have seen, for example, how the life of piety and austerity of Pope Pius V broke with the ostentatious life-style of most of the Renaissance popes.

Our examination of the papacy, however, is more complex than it may seem at first sight. Christian princes looked on the sovereign pontiff as one of their own, especially – as was often the case – when he came from one of the ruling families of Italy. Thus some princes thought that Pius V and Sixtus V, both members of mendicant orders, lacked the breeding and experience required to deal with worldly, political matters. That criticism, however, was somewhat annulled by the Gallican notion that an evangelical humility befitted the successor of Saint Peter – an ideal which Pope Clement VIII espoused.[2]

The way people regarded the papacy was in fact inseparable from the way they perceived the city of Rome itself. That perception was expanded during the course of the sixteenth and seventeenth centuries in several ways. For example, the archaeological excavations of the catacombs, undertaken after their chance discovery on the via Salaria in 1578, provided evidence of the city's historical continuity with the Rome of the martyrs.[3] The popes stirred up popular devotion, not just in Rome but far and wide, by declaring Holy Years – for example, in 1575 and 1600. But they also interspersed the Holy Years with more frequent, extraordinary jubilees (1576, 1578, 1580, etc.). These occasions affected many more people than the pilgrims who flocked to Rome. The faithful throughout Christendom, for example, were able to gain special indulgences during their observance. Anyone who did come to Rome would have been dazzled by the size and splendour of the new basilica of Saint Peter. Originally designed and built to be the largest church in the world, it was enlarged again, to be completed only in 1614 and consecrated by Urban VIII in 1626. It provided a visible, splendid centre for the

2   Alain Tallon, *Conscience nationale et sentiment religieux en France au XVIe siècle* (Paris, 2002), 245, 273.
3   They were vividly described by Antonio Bosio in his *Roma sotterranea* (Rome, 1632 [*sic,* 1635]; repr. 1998).

Roman Church, creating something entirely different from the simple and sober places where Protestants worshipped. Church activities of all types fashioned an urbane, cultural, and religious icon at the service of the ideal of Catholicity.[4]

Seldom had the universal role of the papacy been more to the forefront than when Pope Gregory XIII introduced a revised calendar of dates. In order to correct the erroneous dating of the Julian calendar, Gregory set up an international commission of scientists of whom the best know is the German Jesuit Christoph Clavius. Acting on their calculations, Gregory XIII declared that Friday, 5 October 1582 would henceforth be known as 15 October. For political and religious reasons, however, only Latin Catholic nations accepted the new calendar, with the others awaiting the eighteenth century or even later before doing so.

In 1586 Sixtus V fixed the number of cardinals at seventy. This was consistent with his administrative reorganization of the Roman Curia. The cardinals were the most important cogs in the mechanism of the papacy, even though their importance as counsellors of the pope was in decline after the Council of Trent. The result of these changes was the increased Italianization of the College of Cardinals. Their personalities, their national or political preferences became all-important each time an electoral conclave was called. In their magisterial histories of the popes Leopold von Ranke and Ludwig von Pastor have convincingly demonstrated the tremendous pressure that the ambassadors of the Catholic powers could bring to bear on the cardinal electors.

The "cardinal-nephews" played an important role in the College of Cardinals. Even the scrupulously austere Pius V named one nephew – a Dominican like himself; and, because he trusted him, he even broke his own reformist rules to bestow on him several benefices and to dispense him from residence in his diocese. Another particularly blatant but brilliant example was Cardinal Ludovico Ludovisi, a nephew of Pope Gregory XV.

4   Gérard Labrot, *L'image de Rome: Une arme pour la Contre-Réforme, 1534–1677* (Seyssel [Haute-Savoie], 1987).

The function of Secretary of State, often thought to have been the creation of Charles Borromeo, was in fact inaugurated by Pope Gregory XIII. He did not, however, give the office to his cardinal-nephew Filippo Boncompagni. He gave it instead to Tolomeo Gallio, Cardinal of Como (1526–1607), thus reducing the influence of his own nephew.

Papal nuncios frequently received the cardinal's hat as a reward for good services in states or territories where they had been dispatched. They were often the deciding factors as to whether or not the Tridentine reformation was successfully implanted in those regions. To single out only one of the many resourceful nuncios, we cite Feliciano Ninguarda (1524–1595), a Dominican from the Swiss Grisons region. Fluent in the languages and cultures of both Germany and Italy, he had great success as nuncio in Salzburg and then as a bishop, first in southern Italy and then in Como in the north.

The Princes and Their Bishops

Attempts to implement the Tridentine reforms often brought conflicts between Rome and Catholic nations and states, not to mention tensions between bishops and the public powers in general. The Spanish governor in Milan, for example, opposed the reforming actions there of its bishop, Charles Borromeo. A quarter-century later, a more serious conflict arose between Pope Paul V and the Venetian Republic. Many causes and pretexts could be cited for this dispute, but they all boiled down to the Republic's fierce spirit of independence in both civil and religious matters. In 1606, Paul V excommunicated the Venetian Senate and put the city under interdict, citing violations of clerical immunity as motive for his action. In response, the Venetian authorities put the erudite and biting pen of the Servite priest Paolo Sarpi[5] to use, and forced the local clergy to ignore the pope and to administer the sacraments. They expelled the Jesuits when they refused to obey their orders. The conflict was finally settled through mediation of the French king, but in the end Venice had won without conceding anything to the papacy.

5   See above, p. 44 n18.

It was indeed not uncommon for the political powers to consider themselves as the arbiters of religious reform. They controlled the bishops whose dioceses lay within their territories, and had no intention of ceding that power to Rome. Apart from Spain and Italy, where cathedral chapters maintained the medieval custom of electing their bishops, most episcopal appointments were made by the prince or king with the consent of the Holy See. In France, acting under the Concordat of Bologna (1516) between King Francis I and Pope Leo X, the kings selected bishops and abbots, and the popes would confirm them. Kings often used this concession to reward powerful families or other clients – a situation that prevailed right up to the French Revolution. Still, in making these appointments the king had to bear in mind a large number of complex written and customary laws and territorial exceptions to them, such as precedents and legal systems that had arisen out of past conflicts of interest, especially economic ones. The Holy See, for example, had the right to receive annates, that is, sums equivalent to the first year's revenue from the diocese of the newly appointed bishop.

Rome was not always content simply to confirm automatically every royal nomination. Acting on the Tridentine mandate to reform Catholicism, Gregory XIV decreed in 1591 that an inquest into "the life and morals" of the nominee should be carried out by the papal nuncio. In 1627 Urban VIII established two separate inquests – one into the life of the diocese, the other into the life of the nominee. Each contained thirteen scrutinies, or questions. Little by little, most kings and princes realized that their nominees had to be able to stand up to the criteria in the scrutinies. In 1643 Anne of Austria, regent for her young son King Louis XIV, formally set up a "council of conscience" to nominate worthy candidates for French bishoprics. The evidence suggests that the royal confessor also played a discreet and secret role in the process. Joseph Bergin[6] has demonstrated that between 1589 and 1661 there was no definitive or monolithic "system of production" of French bishops. Even if the corps of bishops was

6   Bergin, *The Making of the French Episcopate, 1589–1661* (New Haven, Conn., 1996).

drawn essentially from the noble class, there was always some social diversity in its composition.

Even so, when examining the lists of bishops from all over Europe, one is struck by the obvious existence of episcopal dynasties, particularly in Italy and France. The best known example is the diocese of Trent, where members of the Madruzzo family, uncle to nephew, succeeded each other four successive times between 1539 and 1658. Sometimes, of course, this questionable system did produce good results, such as when Francis de Sales succeeded his uncle, of whom he had been the coadjutor, as bishop of Geneva; or when Federico Borromeo (1595–1631) succeeded his cousin Charles; or when, in 1571 in the diocese of Carpentras, Giacomo Sacrati, nephew of the reforming bishop Jacopo Sadoleto, was named to succeed the coadjutor Paolo Sadoleto.

Thus, although there were countless instances of familial connections in the choice of bishops, some of these family ties produced effective, even spiritual bishops. In many cases reforming bishops were able to designate or to influence the choice of bishops who would be agents of reform. This was true, for example, in Italy, with Saint Philip Neri; in Portugal, with Bartolomeu a Martyribus; in Poland, with Cardinal Stanislaus Hosius (1504–1579). We often fail to take sufficiently into account the stunning results that a reforming bishop could accomplish. Imagine the spiritual force that a bishop like Luigi de Torres, a disciple of Saint Philip Neri, who was named the archbishop of Monreale (Sicily) in 1591, could bring to his diocese. He once wrote:

> My joy is my spouse [the Church of my diocese]; my throne where I assist at the Divine Office; this altar where I offer the sacrifice to our Lord God; this pulpit from which I sometimes preach; my seminary; the frequent distribution of the Holy Eucharist; the people coming in greater numbers to my church. I take the greatest joy in hearing the instruction of the children in Christian doctrine.[7]

7   Translated and cited by Alphonse Dupront, *Genèses des temps modernes: Rome, les réformes et le Nouveau Monde*, ed. Dominique Julia and Philippe Boutry (Paris, 2001), 219.

Priests and Their Parishes

If one accepts the traditional view that the creation and wide-spread implantation of seminaries was the greatest innovation of the Council of Trent, it is because this institution did finally produce a new priestly ideal and general level of competence – although the notion of "vocation" came only later in the seventeenth century. This enhanced image and status of the Catholic priest was already germinating in the minds of those who wrote and passed the reform decree in the twenty-first session of Trent. They looked to and longed for the day when only men who were sufficiently educated and who had a good moral character would be ordained. The need to understand Latin sufficiently to conduct liturgical services meant that the priest's flock at least looked on him as an educated man. Episcopal visitations of parishes were supposed to verify that every parish priest who was entrusted with the "care of souls" possessed at least a Latin Bible, the diocesan statutes, a source book for homilies, and a confessor's manual. The visitation reports mention frequently, however, the absence of the Bible.

As for his moral life, ecclesiastical celibacy was officially enforced, and priests were forbidden to maintain concubines; but such abuses continued to exist – more in the country than in towns. Priests were not to attend balls or to frequent taverns. On the street they were to wear the clerical garb which, in 1589, Sixtus V specified as a long garment reaching down to the heels of the shoes. In the country or when travelling, however, provision was made for something shorter to be worn.

As for the duties of the parish priest, he was, first of all, charged with the administration of the sacraments. The Council of Trent, following the opinion of Josse Clichtove,[8] decreed that he should have some knowledge of theology and, especially, a basic spiritual formation. He must celebrate the liturgy decently and exactly according to the rituals at his disposition. Catholics were to confess their sins to him at least once each year. The priest was delegated to preach by the bishop, who alone possessed the plenitude of the priesthood and thus

8   See above, p. 60, with n26.

of predication. On Sundays and great feast days the priest was charged with explaining to the people in their own language the Scriptural readings that he had already read in Latin in the celebration of Mass.

The council wanted the priest to have a sufficient income. Thus, the reform of Catholicism could not be carried out without a certain reform of the system of benefices. Each parish was under the sponsorship or patronage of a person (the bishop or a local lay dignitary) or of an institution (an abbey, chapter, or the city). That person or institution had the right to present a candidate for the parish to the bishop of the place, who would confirm the appointment by awarding him the benefice allotted to the parish. The council had also decreed[9] that there be an examination of all candidates. In the early years this discouraged many from applying. The system of holding an open contest when a parish position fell vacant was used only rarely.

Once he was named to a parish, the priest could receive the benefice that was attached to it; but, if he could not reside in the parish, he had to share it with a "perpetual vicar" who carried out the pastor's duties in his absence. He could also count on the "casual," a customary monetary offering, as recompense for celebrating the sacraments. To avoid any scandal of simony, however, he was required constantly to remind the people that sacraments were administered freely without charge. The system of tithing, an ecclesiastical tax calculated on harvests, was regulated by many written or unwritten rules; but it was the cause of many complaints.

The parish priest, especially in villages, exercized authority over local confraternities and over the men of the parish who oversaw its funds and maintenance. He had the duty to see that instruction was carried out by someone capable or to do this himself. He also had responsibility to assist the poor and even the sick. This is why so many priests were also looked on as "healers."

The pastor kept the registry for baptisms, marriages, burials, and – if he observed the Ritual of Pope Paul V – a registry of "the state of souls" containing both positive and negative information about parish

9   Session 24 (11 November 1563), Reform decree 18. See Tanner, *Decrees* 2: *770–2; *Canons and Decrees*, 207–10.

families. He was therefore a truly powerful figure in village society. He was at the centre of a complex system of social and religious associations – usually friendly but sometimes hostile – that made up the church life of post-Tridentine Catholicism.[10]

Parish visitations from the bishop or his representative gave lay people the opportunity to express their opinions about the way the parish was run. In the seventeenth century parish "missions" afforded the chance to evaluate and improve the religious and pastoral ministry that had been born with reformed Catholicism. In effect, it was a ministry which rested heavily on the shoulders of any parish priest who was in daily contact with his flock.

Religious Orders, from Generals to Troops of the Line

The sixteenth century witnessed the founding of a great number of religious orders and congregations which contributed greatly to the spread of Catholic doctrine and renewal. The better known among them, in chronological order of their approval, were the Theatines (1524), the Capuchins (1525), the Barnabites and their feminine branch called the Angelicas of Saint Paul (both in 1533), the Ursulines (1535), the Jesuits (1540), the Oratorians (1565), the "Doctrinaires" (Secular Priests of Christian Doctrine) of César de Bus (1597), the Visitandines (1610), and the Piarists (1617).

The Fathers of the Council of Trent were well aware that the Protestant Reformation originated in priories of religious men, since most of the leading Reformers – Luther, Butzer, and Ochino – had been members of religious orders. It was therefore necessary to assure proper discipline wherever it had been allowed to slip, and to restore responsibility of the bishops over monasteries, convents, and priories in their dioceses. The council's decree of 3–4 December 1563 (Session 25) attempted to discern, for both men's and women's religious orders, how practical, salutary reforms might be accomplished. It concentrated, first, on the abuse of commendatory appointments – giving the direction and the benefices of a monastery or religious order to

---

10 Gabriel Audisio, *Les Français d'hier,* vol. 2: *Des croyants, XVe–XIXe siècle* (Paris, 1996), has described this at some length.

someone who was not a member of that house or order, and dispensing them from the rules and constitutions of the house or order. It was a reform, they realized, that would have to be a gradual one.[11]

The council also took care to regroup small, independent, or dispersed religious congregations into larger and well-organized ones.[12] Canons Regular of Saint Augustine were combined into the Genovéfains centred on the Abbey of Sainte-Geneviève in Paris. Small houses of Benedictine monks in Lorraine were combined into the Congregation of Saint-Vanne. In an attempt to recapture the reforming spirit that, in the sixteenth century, had taken root among the Dominicans in France and in Franciscans generally, the Holy See gave encouragement and support to leaders of observant movements, such as the Recollects in the Franciscan Order and Father Sébastien Michaelis of the Dominicans.

The Jesuits and the Capuchins were the two orders of men who provided the larger part of the priests needed for the reform of Catholicism. Chapter Twelve will highlight the importance of the Society of Jesus which, with a cadre of remarkable and often heroic men, took the lead in re-Catholicizing Europe and in taking the faith to foreign lands.

The Capuchins ("Friars Minor of the Eremitical Life") survived serious difficulties[13] in their initial years in Italy. They received strong encouragement from Pope Gregory XIII in 1574 to labour in both domestic and foreign missions. In that same year a community of Italian Capuchins opened a house in Lyons, where they had immediate success. They knew how to pray with the people, and, by effective preaching backed up with public devotions, they were able to satisfy the thirst of their flock for the supernatural. They initiated the Forty Hours Devotion, consisting of prolonged adoration of the Blessed Sacrament. Their reputation for sanctity, austerity, and simplicity drew popular support in Savoy and French-speaking Switzerland. In the Aosta valley in Italy they struggled mightily against the Prot-

---

11 See Tanner, *Decrees* 2: *783, ch. 21.
12 See Tanner, *Decrees* 2: *779, ch. 8.
13 Notably the defection of their vicar-general, Bernardino Ochino, to Protestantism.

estants' "venom of heresy."[14] Their achievements in these missionary campaigns were chronicled in the mid-seventeenth century by Father Charles de Genève in his book *Sacred Trophies*,[15] which portrays their success with "the weapons of the Holy War": the catechism, the confession of sins, and a number of devotional practices – all under the protection of the "Empress of the Universe" (their name for the Blessed Virgin Mary).

Religious Women, from Observance of the Cloister to Works of Charity

The Council of Trent thought it best to restore and assure strict enclosure for nuns, at least as far as it was physically possible. In short, nuns should never leave their convent, and no one not a nun should ever be allowed to enter it. In its insistence that this rule be "carefully established and perfectly observed,"[16] the council sought to protect women religious from their families and acquaintances, who often looked on the convent as an annex to the family home where they had certain rights. If that practice were to continue, the convent would never be free of a certain worldly spirit.

The council also established a minimum age of sixteen years. Girls of that age, it was thought, could intelligently and freely choose to enter a convent, while those who did not choose it could not be forced. In the council's attempts to regulate financial stability for convents and monasteries, radical poverty was never the intention. At the same time, the Fathers wanted anyone in convents or monasteries to live simply and without extravagance.[17] For their spiritual well-being nuns should have access to the sacraments of Penance and Holy Eucharist at least once every month.[18]

14   The expression is that of Bernard Dompnier, *Le venin de l'hérésie: image du protestantisme et combat catholique au XVIIe siècle* (Paris, 1985).
15   Charles de Genève, *Les Trophées sacrés, ou missions des Capucins en Savoie ...*, ed. Félix Tisserand (Lausanne, 1976).
16   *CT* 9: 1080, ch. 9. See also Tanner, *Decrees* 2: *777–8, ch. 5.
17   *CT* 9: 1080, ch. 2. See also Tanner, *Decrees* 2: *776–7, ch. 2.
18   *CT* 9: 1082, ch. 2. See also Tanner, *Decrees* 2: *779–80, ch. 10.

Angélique Arnaud, the young mother-superior of the great convent of Port-Royal in Paris, tried to enforce the rule of cloister by closing the convent to her own influential family.[19] An opposite action had occurred in 1576 when Catherine de Ricci,[20] the superior of the Dominican convent in Prato, Italy, insisted that her convent of Third Order Regulars had never been intended to be cloistered. She reasoned that the Order's tradition of mendicancy could not be maintained if the sisters were enclosed. In fact, the enforcement of enclosure proved difficult to uphold in almost every type of convent. The simple fact was that many of the measures required to reform Catholicism demanded charitable workers and teachers, and religious women were best suited to provide them. Finding solutions for those needs made it necessary to negotiate and to mitigate the rules.

A good example is the Ursulines,[21] who became especially important in educating young Catholic girls. The life's journey of Angela Merici (1474–1540) had led her to enter, first of all, the Third Order Franciscans. She later came under the influence of Philip Neri and the Oratory. She was already fifty-one years old in 1535 when she founded the Company of Saint Ursula in Brescia. She first organized small groups of consecrated virgins in their own neighbourhoods, and later combined them into larger communities under the patronage of the Saint Ursula and the martyrs of Cologne. They took vows to perform works of mercy – particularly to educate young girls. Angela's intuition in this was crucial to the reform of Catholicism: who other than those same young girls, when they had grown to be adults and mothers of families, would be better placed to assure their own children a solid Christian formation?

The Ursulines were ratified by Rome in 1543, just three years after the death of their foundress. They would later be taken in hand and strengthened by Charles Borromeo, who called them to Milan in 1565

---

19 The description of this incident, known as the "Journée du Guichet" ("Day of the Grille"), is a celebrated passage in Charles-Augustin Sainte-Beuve, *Port-Royal* (Paris, 1840–1859), 1: 100–15.
20 (1522–1590). She was later canonized a saint in 1746.
21 Philippe Annaert, *Les collèges au féminin: Les Ursulines; Enseignement et vie consacrée aux XVIIe et XVIIIe siècles* (Namur, 1992).

and modified their Rule. From there they spread throughout northern Italy and then into the Comtat Venaissin, with its capital at Carpentras, and Provence, from where their foundations spread throughout France. Because the Ursulines asked only a modest dowry from the families of their novices, they could recruit many women from the financially lower levels of society.

The Ursulines nevertheless found themselves faced with the difficult choice of whether to obey the strict enclosure legislated by the Council of Trent or to operate as apostolic communities outside the traditional monastic model. This second solution was chosen by one branch of the Ursulines led by Anne de Xainctonge (1565–1621) at Dôle in Franche-Comté, and it was approved by the archbishop of Besançon in 1604. Other similar congregations followed suit, such as the Society of Notre-Dame in Bordeaux in 1607. Jeanne de Lestonnac (1556–1640), a niece of Michel de Montaigne, tried to instill a Jesuit orientation into her community of Ursuline nuns.

The majority of Ursulines, however, accepted a mitigated rule of cloistered life. With the help of intelligent dispensations from choir and strict austerities they were able to carry on their charism of education. Beginning in 1612 some communities began taking a fourth vow: to teach young girls, and in this way they established an extensive school system. Their main goal was to give young girls the skills to support themselves and to be the strong anchors of Christian families. As a result, the Ursulines played a strategic social role in the society of the Ancien Régime.

The nuns of the Visitation Sainte-Marie[22] underwent a similar evolution. Although their founders – Francis de Sales and Jeanne de Chantal – gave to their communities a traditional contemplative way of life, they also instilled in their nuns a charism for looking after the poor.

A New Era of the "Pious Layman"

Pious lay people had never been lacking in the Church. In the fifteenth century, however, especially in the Low Countries and

---

22 For the Visitandines, see above, p. 106.

Flanders, the "devotion" of certain groups of lay persons – known as confraternities or sodalities – contributed greatly to the reform of Catholicism, and this movement continued in the period after the Council of Trent. The historian Louis Châtellier[23] has pointed out the social and religious importance of some of them, particularly groups ·devoted to the Virgin Mary that were founded by the Jesuits. By the seventeenth century they had formed an extensive network of lay devotees who were committed Catholics.

One of the first of these was a kind of confraternity founded in 1563 at the Jesuit college in Rome by Jean Leunis, a priest from Liège. It was dedicated to honouring the Virgin Mary. At first only a modest project designed to gather students together for pious devotions, it grew into an extensive program of Christian life. In 1565 Leunis founded a similar confraternity at the Collège de Clermont, the Jesuit college in Paris. There, too, it was a success, and it led to the establishment of similar groups in many other places. Father Franz Coster founded Marian "sodalities" in Douai, Cologne, and the Low Countries, and composed formal and detailed statutes for them.[24] Some prominent Jesuits, Antonio Possevino, Edmond Auger, Juan Maldonato, and Peter Canisius at Fribourg, were members and leaders of this movement.

Sodalities[25] were encouraged to hold public manifestations in honour of the Blessed Virgin Mary. Such visible displays of devotion aided greatly in recruiting members for the sodalities. They evolved from simple college groups to include men from diverse classes and professions. Later some groups split off according to their different trades, social status, and other common traits, but they all continued

23 Châtellier, *The Europe of the Devout: The Catholic Reformation and the For-mation of a New Society*, trans. Jean Birrell (Cambridge; New York; Paris, 1989), 49–66; originally published as *L'Europe des dévots* (Paris, 1987).
24 Coster, *Libellus sodalitatis, hoc est, Christianarum institutionum libri quin-que, in gratiam sodalitatis B. Virginis Mariae* (Antwerp; Ingolstadt, 1586; many reprints).
25 The term "Sodality" was more widely used in English-speaking areas. Current historiography prefers the earlier latinate term "confraternity" for the similar groups of lay persons that had flourished in Italy, France, and Spain since the fifteenth century.

to operate under the same principles and with the same organization. Marian sodalities were therefore a kind of blueprint for a greater pastoral role of lay people in the Church. Their devotion spread and gave rise to Catholic religious practices that lasted into the twentieth century: "Morning prayer, evening examination of conscience, confession twice a month, and frequent reception of Holy Communion – these became over the years normal practices in the common upbringing of Catholic families."[26]

Still other forms of lay associations sprung up and proved to be a sign of the vitality of the Catholic reformation. In some places confraternities and particularly penitential associations practiced ecstatic penitential devotions. In Avignon, as these latter kinds of groups grew more numerous, the Church tried to redirect their enthusiasm towards more interior forms of piety.[27]

The reform of Catholicism owes much to this large and diverse range of devout, even zealous, lay people. Formed in piety and committed to the communal and public manifestation of its importance to them, they made personal and public prayer an essential part of their lives. They became a solid basis for Catholic action in the world.

26 Châtellier, *The Europe of the Devout*, 254.
27 Marc Venard, *Réforme protestante, réforme catholique dans la province d'Avignon, XVIe siècle* (Paris, 1993).

CHAPTER TWELVE

Reconquest and Spiritual Renewal

The post-Tridentine Church continued to maintain a defensive position against the spread of Protestantism. Chairs in controversial theology were established in Catholic universities where, even though debate could sometimes be intense, an irenic approach generally prevailed. Robert Bellarmine held such a chair in the Jesuit Roman College. In a much different, violent way, Catholics fought during the nearly forty years of the Wars of Religion (1561–1598) to keep France Catholic. Later, in the German Empire, similar warfare, in which both religion and politics played a part, broke out during the Thirty Years War (1618–1648) between Catholic and Protestant cities, states, and princes.

The reform of Catholicism moved beyond defensive postures to adopt a more dynamic and militant stance. The victory against the Turks at Lepanto was the symbol of a new-found vigour, a collective confidence that fulfilled dreams of winning back lands and peoples that had been lost. Some of those dreams were to be realized, but others were not. The crushing defeat of Catholic Spain's "Invincible Armada" in 1588 ended the dream of re-Catholicizing England.

In this final chapter we would like to illustrate how the militant Catholicism that had been articulated by the Council of Trent was redeployed in new missionary, cultural, and spiritual dimensions. In the minds of men and women in real situations this redeployment both fulfilled and transformed the council's intentions.

In the late fifteenth and early sixteenth century the papacy recognized and confirmed the maritime hegemony of Portugal and Spain when it confided to those two nations a monopoly in evangelizing (and thus in colonizing) lands newly discovered "or yet to be discovered" – that is, Asia, Africa, and the Americas.[1] Even at the height of the Protestant Reformation, the firm control by those two

---

1   These were provisions of the Treaty of Tordesillas (June 1494).

Catholic powers of their own destinies and of so much of the world remained unchallenged by any Protestant state for over a century. Catholic France joined the two colonial powers with the arrival of French Jesuits in Canada in 1610. They were followed five years later by Capuchins and Franciscan Recollects. Even if only slowly, the structures and the habits of Catholic reform became established in far-off lands.

Temporal Victories and Spiritual Conquest

With the exception of Brazil, which the Treaty of Tordesillas relegated to Portugal, Central and South America became colonies of Spain. Some Spanish theologians and Church officials were concerned, however, with the legitimacy of conquering inhabited lands and especially with the effect it would have on the native peoples. Pope Paul III's bull *Sublimis Deus* (1537) may have planted the seed of that concern.[2] Lewis Hanke[3] has argued that the history of disputation contains few examples as open, passionate, and public as the arguments put forth by the university theologian Francisco de Vitoria (1492–1546) and by the passionate advocate of the American "Indians," Bartolomeo de Las Casas (1474–1566), who argued for a peaceful, not a forced, evangelization.[4]

But the missionary task, on the one hand, and colonization and profit, on the other, had opposite aims. All things considered, however, the reform of Catholicism after Trent did at least help to restrain some of the most flagrant colonizing abuses. The pastoral literature and the documents of synods held in Mexico, in particular the one in 1585, illustrate both the important efforts made and the limits of this approach.[5]

2   *The Sublime God* is considered to be the most important papal pronouncement on the dignity of the native peoples. Some have seen it as an open condemnation of slavery.

3   Hanke, *The Spanish Struggle for Justice in the Conquest of America* (Philadelphia, 1949).

4   Hanke, *Bartolomé de las Casas: An Interpretation of his Life and Writings* (The Hague, 1951).

5   Enrique D. Dussel, *A History of the Church in Latin America: Colonialism to Liberation (1492–1979)*, trans. and revised by Alan Neely (Grand Rapids, Mich., 1981).

The Jesuits took a more radical tack in solving the colonization problem. Taking their cue from what Las Casas had learned in Guatemala and from certain initiatives of the Franciscans, they implemented on a wide scale what they called Reductions – colonies where native people could be "led back" to Christianity and civilization. This was a totally new experiment, never tried anywhere. It began just at the time when the reform of Catholicism was taking root in Europe, and it lasted for a century and a half. The first village of this type was set up for the Guarani tribe in 1610 by two Italian Jesuits, Simón Maceta and José Cataldino, who received permission to place their experiment directly under the jurisdiction of the king of Spain. This adaptation of Jesuit missionary methods was not done for the sake of inculturation but, rather, of preventing the Spanish colonials from abusing the native peoples. In the end, its results were uneven and only partially successful.[6]

Saint Francis Xavier died in 1552 without having been able to take Christianity into China. But he and other missionaries had crisscrossed many provinces of Asia, from India to Japan and into Indonesia, and had made a good start in converting the people of the Philippines. The Dominicans, not content to rest on their laurels there, turned their vision, as had Francis Xavier, to the Chinese mainland. This is why the first book ever printed in the Philippines was set in Chinese characters. Written by Juan Cobo (1546–1592), his *Apology for True Religion* (1593) was an initiation into the Catholic faith. The college of Santo Tomás, from which later grew the university bearing that name, was founded in Manila in 1611.

After Jesuit missionaries had finally managed to enter the Chinese mainland, Matteo Ricci (1552–1610)[7] gained access to the Chinese literate class by using a manual of Christian doctrine printed in Chinese (1603) similar to the one prepared by Cobo. In order to be

6   For "a personal account of the founding and early years of the Jesuit Paraguay reductions," see *The Spiritual Conquest Accomplished by the Religious of the Society of Jesus in the Provinces of Paraguay, Paraná, Uruguay, and Tape,* written by Antonio Ruiz de Montoya (1585–1652), trans. C.J. McNaspy, John P. Leonard, and Martin E. Palmer (St Louis, Mo., 1993).

7   Étienne Ducornet, *Matteo Ricci, le lettré d'Occident* (Paris, 1992).

able to communicate with the Chinese people, Ricci and his companions chose a mode of Christian life that was open to Confucian thought rather than to Buddhism. In 1615 Pope Paul V granted to the French Jesuit Nicolas Trigault (1577–1628) the exceptional privilege of celebrating the Roman liturgy in the Chinese language of his literate entourage – something the Council of Trent had prohibited. That privilege was to be withdrawn twenty-five years later when the famous quarrel over a "Chinese rite" broke out.[8]

That same ruling also touched, but only somewhat later, the missionary initiatives that an Italian Jesuit, Roberto de Nobili (1577–1656), had taken in southern India. Having learned Sanskrit and the Tamil language, he lived in the style of a Hindu penitent (*sannyasi*) and translated an explanation of the principal articles of the Christian faith into those languages. When some Brahmans wanted to convert to Christianity, Nobili did not ask them to forsake their way of life, and Pope Gregory XV approved his decision (1623).

It is therefore clear that, although they were later criticized for paternalism and theological syncretism, the methods of those Catholic missionaries – especially the Jesuits – were extraordinarily bold and resourceful. They manifested a renewed Catholic vitality for evangelizing foreign lands that was put under the aegis of the *Propaganda Fide*, a Congregation specially created for that purpose.

The Reconquest of Europe

By the time the Council of Trent approached its end, extensive parts of central Europe had either crossed over to Protestantism or had been conquered by the Ottoman Empire, while immense Russian territories remained under the control of the Orthodox czar. The Holy Roman Empire in Germany had ratified the Peace of Augsburg (1555), which stated that each territory would adopt the religion of its prince. It was a compromise formula which did not please anyone. It had to allow many exceptions, because it had been formulated with

---

8   [René] Étiemble, *Les Jésuites en Chine (1552–1773): La querelle des rites* (Paris, 1966). For a general history in English, see Liam Matthew Brockey, *Journey to the East: The Jesuit Mission to China, 1579–1724* (Cambridge, Mass., 2007).

only Catholicism and Lutheranism in mind and did not take into account the growing presence of Calvinism in central and eastern Europe. Over this extensive Empire, which was a veritable mosaic of languages, nationalities, and juridical and social differences, reigned the Catholic sovereign. Starting from that central fact, it was natural that attempts to regain certain territories for Catholicism would be made. We shall consider three examples.

The first involves Styria, located in present-day Austria near Hungary and Croatia. Because it was one of the hereditary Habsburg states and its official religion was Catholicism, the Peace of Augsburg should juridically have guaranteed it remain Catholic. But, because Protestantism had made significant inroads there, the Archduke Charles II (1564–1590) granted religious freedom to Protestant nobles and bourgeois for the period 1572–1578. When a papal nuncio arrived in the Styrian capital city of Graz, however, the archduke began to apply non-violent methods of enforcing the Catholic reform, such as the censorship of books and surveillance of preaching. Gradually the Roman Church began to regain both souls and territory, and the reconquest of Styria was an accomplished fact by the end of the century.

Hungary is our second example. In 1526, a great part of it had fallen either under the direct control or indirect protection of the Turks. The Habsburgs reigned only in the remaining part known as "royal" Hungary, where a religious rivalry between Catholics, Lutherans, and Calvinists was in full ferment. The Jesuits devised a pastoral strategy designed to convert everyone back to Catholicism. Three archbishops of Esztergom – Miklós Oláh (1493–1568), Ferenc Forgách (1564–1615), and especially Péter Pázmány (1570–1637), successfully kept the Catholic minority faithful, and were greatly helped in this goal by getting all the religious houses and churches built by Catholics restored to their control. As the seventeenth century progressed, however, conversions from one Church to another slowed and finally stabilized. The polarization of Hungary's population vis-à-vis Habsburg rule played a role in this, as did the constant vigilance to the ever present menace of the Ottoman Turks.

Bohemia, on the contrary, provides an example of a more successful Catholic reconquest. A variety of persons faithful to the Hussite tradition were, of course, always present and would not convert. Their largest group, known as neo-Utraquists, had also been inspired by Luther. They adhered to the *Bohemian Confession* of 1575 which was reaffirmed in 1609.[9] Catholic Bohemians were energized by the "personnel" of reform, particularly the religious orders. The Jesuits had been brought to Prague by Peter Canisius, and the Capuchins were also very active. The Premonstratensian abbey of Strahov in Prague made a special contribution to Catholic reform with its famous library developed by the Abbot Jan Lohel (1549–1622). After the arrival of the Catholic court of Rudolf II, a papal nuncio was appointed to Prague in 1584. Although he was adept in coordinating the various elements of Catholic renewal, its expansion and even its continued presence were to be put at risk by grave political events.

In 1609, Rudolf II had been forced to issue a "Letter of Majesty" granting religious freedom to all his Bohemian subjects. The fact that it was not fully implemented in ecclesiastical territories provoked the celebrated "defenestration of Prague" in 1618, when two Catholic delegates to a parley were thrown from a high window into a moat below. Religious toleration broke down; and, after Ferdinand II was elected emperor, a civil war followed which mobilized Catholic troops. Inspired by the mystical visions of the Carmelite friar Dominic of Jesus-Maria and horrified by the incidents of iconoclasm which he had witnessed, these troops won the battle of White Mountain on 8 November 1620. It was a decisive and symbolic victory; and, just as the defeat of the Turkish navy at Lepanto had been attributed to Our Lady of the Rosary, so was this Catholic reconquest attributed to the Virgin Mary. Some compared the victory to a new Crusade.

Farther east[10] in the Polish-Lithuanian Confederation, a conflict in Ukraine and Byelorussia ("Belarus" today) between the hierarchy of the Ruthenian Church and members of powerful lay confraternities broke out. It followed the creation in 1589 of the patriarchate of Moscow by Jeremiah II (1572–1594), patriarch of Constantinople,

9   Based largely on the Augsburg Confession of 1530, it subscribed to the Lutheran position on justification and the Calvinist interpretation of the Eucharist.
10   Olivier Chaline, *La reconquête catholique de l'Europe centrale, XVIe–XVIIe siècle* (Paris, 1998).

after extreme pressure exerted by Boris Godunov. Beginning in 1577, Catholic resistance had been awakened by the Jesuit theologian and missionary Peter Skarga of Vilnius, Lithuania. Certain Ruthenian bishops sought to return to union with Rome predicated on the agreement that had been reached at the Council of Florence (1439) but later rejected by the populace. Despite the differences in ecclesiologies between the Roman Curia and the two bishops who were sent as envoys to Rome, the Union was agreed upon and ratified by the members of a synod held at Brest-Litovsk in 1596. Pope Clement VIII agreed to allow the Byzantine liturgy and ecclesiastical discipline to remain in use. Despite serious opposition which led to his assassination, Archbishop Josaphat Kuncewicz (1580–1623) of Polosk worked to recognize and strengthen the new union with Rome by an interior reform of the Ukrainian Church.[11]

At the other end of continental Europe, not far from the English Channel, English Catholics ("recusants") were likewise preparing themselves for a spiritual reconquest of their land, a goal for which the Jesuit Edmund Campion (1540–1581) was martyred by beheading on a charge of treason. The formation of future priests who were likewise ready to risk their lives on missions to England could only safely take place on the Continent. William Allen (1532–1594) was the principal architect of these theological colleges for recusant emigrants. Along with other former Oxford students he set up one such college at Douai in northern France in 1568, another in Rome in 1575, and a third in Valladolid in Castile in 1589.

It is interesting to see how quickly English recusants came to the conviction that they should have a translation of the Bible in their own language,[12] free from doctrinal errors, with which they might confidently confront their Anglican adversaries. Translation of the New Testament was entrusted to Gregory Martin, who finished it in

---

11   See Oscar Halecki, *From Florence to Brest (1439–1596)* (Rome; New York, 1958; repr. North Haven, Conn., 1968).

12   Three English Bibles were already in print – those of William Tyndale (1525), Miles Coverdale (1535), and the so-called Geneva Bible (1560). All three were considered to contain Protestant readings or interpretations. The King James "Authorized Version" did not appear until 1611.

1582, the year of his death. The Old Testament appeared only in 1609. This English-language version, known as the Douai-Rheims Bible, was a translation from the Latin Vulgate, although its annotations referred to readings from the Greek and Hebrew. It drew sharp criticism from Protestant scholars, most of them graduates of Cambridge University. Is it not worthy of note that the English recusant desire to reconvert their land managed to combine a humanist dimension of biblical scholarship with the Protestant demand for vernacular access to the Word of God?

A Catholic Culture

At this point we might ask: did the reform of Catholicism give rise to a distinct culture? Our answer is, "Yes, it did," even if it is not always easy to distinguish its different elements. The place of the Bible in the life of Catholics at the end of the sixteenth and in the seventeenth century is a case in point, and it forces us to think beyond what we often hear about this. Most people presume that Catholics of that time were denied access to the Bible, first, by the use of Latin in the liturgy and, second, by a reluctance in the Church to allow them to read it in their own language. That is only partly true. No matter their level of education or culture, Catholics were familiar with Bible paraphrases and summaries that were recommended and used by Church authorities. Their catechisms used and referred to Bible texts and stories. The sermons they heard were often explanations of the biblical texts appointed for the day's Mass. Thus, although Catholics did not in general read the Bible text directly, their culture contained a large measure of input from it. Contemporary historians have studied this question in order to discern whether this Catholic culture reached only the elite, to whom it was indeed more readily accessible, or whether it also affected the lives of the common people. Looking at this from different vantage points, three French historians – Louis Châtellier, who investigates "the religion of the poor," Gabriel Audisio, and Marc Venard – all contribute elements of an answer that permit us to envisage a Catholic culture that was inseparable from the daily experience of Catholics.

There is one way of approaching Catholic culture that was easily accessible to all: the array of images that pervaded Catholic places of worship and even public spaces. The culture of reformed Catholicism is figuratively encapsulated in religious art. The Catholic experience was situated between the two extremes of Protestant iconoclasm, traces of which are still present, and divinization of icons, which was only rarely encountered in Catholic worship. The Catholic experience embraced a panoply of painted and sculpted works which, although mostly rejected by other confessions, helped many Catholics assimilate a religious element into their daily lives.

The Council of Trent dealt with the question of images in the restricted context of the cult of saints. The decree dealing with prayer to saints and veneration of saints, and with their relics and images, was voted in Session 25 (3–4 December 1563).[13] At first it offers only generalities about keeping clear of heterodoxy, about the danger of errors in representing saints, and about avoiding superstition in using images. Only at the end of the century, with treatises by Gabriele Paleotti[14] and Johannes de Molanus[15] and especially with the *De pictura sacra* of Federico Borromeo,[16] were more elaborate presentations of Catholic doctrine made and practical norms offered. In the baroque era that followed, pictorial and sculpted images lavishly filled sacred spaces. They were intended and presented to glorify reformed Catholicity and to invite the people to contemplate its meaning in their lives. Pushed to this aesthetic extreme, reformed Catholicism found its ultimate form in depicting sanctity in such a way that the spiritual transfigures the physical without denying or abolishing its reality.

13 See Tanner, *Decrees* 2: *774–6.
14 Paleotti, *Discorso intorno alle imagini sacre et profane, diviso in cinque libri* (Bologna, 1582).
15 Molanus, *De picturis et imaginibus sacris* (Louvain, 1570; repr. Ingolstadt, 1594). For a recent French translation, see *Traité des saintes images,* ed. and trans. François Boespflug et al. (Paris, 1996). Molanus strongly promoted the use of religious art, but he demanded it be free of the myths that frequently pervaded medieval art.
16 (Milan, 1624). Borromeo's own Italian version has recently been issued: *Della pittura sacra,* ed. B. Agosti (Pisa, 1994). A year after publication of the Latin version, Federico Borromeo founded the great Biblioteca Ambrosiana in Milan. More than just a magnificent library, it also houses an extensive collection of religious art.

Conclusion

The chronological limits of this book, beginning around 1480 and extending to the years just after 1620, span a period that begins with the reformist preaching of Savonarola and ends with the death of Saint Francis de Sales, the battle of White Mountain, and the creation of the Congregation for the Propagation of the Faith in 1622. We have therefore gone from prophetic but unfulfilled yearnings for a return to the ideal of a purified Church to the establishment of solid and pragmatic decrees and institutions designed to strengthen the faithful people in their universal (not ministerial) priesthood and in their devotional life. We have witnessed the failure of Savonarola's Florentine "Republic of Jesus Christ," but have also witnessed militant conquests inspired by mystical visions and culminating in organized, courageous, and often heroic sacrifices to announce the Gospel of Christ to the farthest corners of the world.

Thus were set in motion, in the space of a century and a half, the three dimensions of a reformed Catholicism: the prophetic, the pastoral, and the political. If the prophetic voices were muted in the sixteenth century, they took other forms in mystical longing and ecstasy, in spiritual canticles and the paradoxes of sanctity. Traditional theology – examined, affirmed, and revised by the Council of Trent – served henceforth pastoral and sacramental practice which found its productive way amidst the decrees of reform and renewal that sometimes seemed to be in disarray. After emerging from the Great Schism and conciliarism, the Church was once again a force in the world. It still worked closely with secular powers, but it perceived that Christendom had been transformed into Christianity and even, in many ways and places, into Catholicism.

Historians of the sixteenth century have rightly put the spotlight on the phenomenon of confessionalization which took place in both Protestantism and Catholicism. Nevertheless, we purposely began our historical survey early enough so that we might perceive the common roots of all the movements of reform; and we have ended it late enough to assure our arrival at a point in history where matters affecting its own good were decided, integrated, and implemented by the Catholic Church acting separately from other Churches.

It would be wrong, however, to imagine that the Roman Church saw its Catholicity simply as one of many sects. On the contrary, the renewed Catholic Church in the early modern world sensed, lived, and preached her global reach. With her reconquest of lands and her cosmic vision (alluded to by Paul Claudel in his *Le soulier de satin*), the Catholic Church lives on the universal stage, from Prague to Tangiers and Japan, on land and on sea. In Rome, St Peter's Basilica expresses this in its own way: vertically by Bernini's baldachino (1624), in which Yves Bonnefoy has perceived the artist's experience of divine transcendence[1]; and horizontally in St Peter's Square, where the same artist's later colonnade draws in and welcomes the world.

But it was principally by its theology that Catholicity was reaffirmed. If humanists – beginning with Erasmus – had had their way, the different Churches would have been able to be reconciled and to agree on a minimalist Credo, a *via media* independent of the subtleties of scholastic theology. Instead, the Roman Church chose a full, detailed Credo which enshrined her dogmas, her definitions, and her spirituality, and through it she enforced her discipline. Yet, despite its will and its attempts to be prudent, the Council of Trent issued many rather dense texts which, inevitably open to interpretation, already contained, from the very time they were approved, the seeds of future quarrels. The council's theology would seem at least to have this much in common with humanism: its devotion and its learning are both imbued with a joyful optimism that is in dialogue with the ancient Fathers and sometimes even with modernity. Still, not wishing to lose any part of its Latin tradition, Catholicism also retained a large measure of Augustinian theology with its tragic dimension of rejecting those who know not God and those who, through sin, have detached themselves from Him and from the Church. Thus, starting in the very period we have studied, the partisans of free will and of grace began

---

1   Bonnefoy, *Rome, 1630: L'horizon du premier baroque; suivi de Un des siècles du culte des images* (Paris, 1994), 18.

to face off. The quarrel *de auxiliis* between Dominicans and Jesuits,[2] which was not resolved but only postponed by a 1607 papal order that chose neither side, was only the prelude to the even greater theological debates between Catholics of the seventeenth century. Still, one of the hallmarks of that century was that very coexistence of opposites which found resolution only because both sides were centred on Christ.

The reform movement in the sixteenth century restored the credibility of the Roman Church and enabled it to live in a kind of equilibrium for at least several decades. This became possible when the Council of Trent agreed to conjoin doctrine and discipline, theology and practice, contemplation and action, and perhaps – even if this seems paradoxical to some – the temporal and the spiritual. In any case, the reform of Catholicism was able to draw together the reality of the profane with the demands of the sacred. It was a precarious equilibrium, indeed, especially when faced with the threat of ever new and different forms of humanism which encircled it, then infiltrated it, and finally laid siege to it. Still, the reform of Catholicism that we have studied gave rise to a culture, a way of life, which had both depth and breadth, and many aspects of it are still perceptible today. That history and that culture of Catholicism, which many Catholics today hold dear, have endured – if not as a model then surely as a legacy.

---

2   The debate continued the unresolved question begun earlier in the century between Protestants and Catholics which gave its name to the whole dispute: the *auxilia* (different modes of help) afforded by divine grace and the joining of efficacious grace with human free will.

Select Bibliography

This Select Bibliography contains the principal sources on which the author has drawn. The translator has added to it similar monographs and documents published in English. For sources documenting particular facets of the text, see the General Bibliography which follows this one.

Bireley, Robert. *The Refashioning of Catholicism, 1450–1700: A Reassessment of the Counter Reformation.* Washington, D.C.: The Catholic University of America Press, 1999.

Cameron, Euan K. *The European Reformation.* Oxford: Clarendon Press, 1991.

Canons and Decrees of the Council of Trent. Ed. and trans. Henry Joseph Schroeder. St Louis, Mo.; London: B. Herder Book Co., 1941. Repr. Rockford, Ill.: Tan Books and Publishers, 1978. [= *Canons and Decrees.*]

The Catholic Reformation: Savonarola to Ignatius Loyola; Reform in the Church, 1495–1540. Ed. John C. Olin. New York; Evanston, Ill.: Harper & Row, 1969. Repr. New York: Fordham Univ. Press, 1992. [English translations of primary sources.] [= Olin.]

Concilium Tridentinum: diariorum, actorum, epistularum, tractatuum nova collectio. Ed. Societas Goerresiana. 13 vols. Freiburg-im-Breisgau: Herder, 1963–1967. [= *CT.*]

The Counter-Reformation: The Essential Readings. Ed. David M. Luebke. Malden, Mass.; Oxford: Blackwell, 1999. [A collection of nine essays.]

DeMolen, Richard L., ed. *Religious Orders of the Catholic Reformation: In Honor of John C. Olin on his Seventy-Fifth Birthday.* New York: Fordham University Press, 1994. [A collection of nine articles.]

Early Modern Catholicism: Essays in Honour of John W. O'Malley, S.J. Ed. Kathleen M. Comerford and Hilmar M. Pabel. Toronto; Buffalo: University of Toronto Press, 2001. [A collection of seventeen articles by different authors.]

Evennett, H. Outram. *The Spirit of the Counter-Reformation*. Ed. John Bossy. Cambridge: Cambridge University Press, 1968. Repr. Notre Dame, Ind.: University of Notre Dame Press, 1970, 1975. [Original subtitle: The Birkbeck Lectures in Ecclesiastical History Given in the University of Cambridge in May 1951.]

Febvre, Lucien. "The Origins of the French Reformation: A Badly-put Question?" Trans. K. Folka. In *A New Kind of History, from the Writings of Lucien Febvre*, ed. Peter Burke, pp. 44–107. Harper Torchbooks. New York; Evanston, Ill.: Harper & Row, 1973. [Originally published as "Une question mal posée: les origines de la Réforme française et le problème des causes de la Réforme," *Revue Historique* 159 (1929): 1–73. Repr. in Lucien Febvre, *Au coeur religieux du XVIe siècle*, Bibliothèque générale de l'école pratique des hautes études 6 (Paris: S.E.V.P.E.N., 1957; 2nd ed. 1968; repr. 1983), pp. 3–70.]

Hsia, Ronald Po-chia. *The World of Catholic Renewal, 1540–1770*. New Approaches to European History 12. Cambridge; New York: Cambridge University Press, 1998. 2nd ed. 2005.

—, ed. *A Companion to the Reformation World*. Blackwell Companions to European History. Malden, Mass.: Blackwell, 2004, 2006. [A collection of 29 chapters, all by different authors.]

Imbart de La Tour, Pierre. *Les origines de la Réforme*. 4 vols. Paris: Hachette, 1905–1935.

Janelle, Pierre. *The Catholic Reformation*. 1949. Milwaukee, Wis.: Bruce Publishing Co., 1963.

Jedin, Hubert. *Catholic Reformation or Counter-Reformation?* Trans. David M. Luebke. In *The Counter-Reformation: The Essential Readings*, ed. David M. Luebke, pp. 19–46. Blackwell Essential Readings in History. Malden, Mass.; Oxford: Blackwell, 1999. [Originally published as *Katholische Reformation oder Gegenreformation? Ein Versuch zur Klärung der Begriffe nebst einer Jubiläumsbetrachtung über das Trienter Konzil*. Lucerne: Josef Stocker, 1946.] [Italian translation: *Riforma cattolica o Controriforma? Tentativo di chiarimento dei concetti con riflessioni sul Concilio di Trento*. Trans. Marola Guarducci. Brescia: Morcelliana, 1957. Many reprints.]

—. *A History of the Council of Trent*. Trans. Ernest Graf. 2 vols. London: Nelson, 1957. [Originally published as *Geschichte des Konzils von Trient*. 4 vols. Freiburg-im-Breisgau: Herder, 1949. Only the first two volumes have been translated from the German.]

Mansi, Giovanni-Domenico, Philippe Labbé, Gabriel Cossart, Niccolò Coleti, Jean-Baptiste Martin, and Louis Petit, eds. *Sacrorum conciliorum nova et amplissima collectio* ... . 53 vols. in 58. Florence; Venice: Antonio Zatta, 1759–1798. Repr. Paris; Leipzig; Arnhem: Welter, 1903–1927. [= Mansi.]

Minnich, Nelson H. *The Catholic Reformation: Council, Churchmen, Controversies*. Aldershot, Hants.; Brookfield, Vt.: Variorum, 1993. [A collection of previously published articles.]

—. *The Fifth Lateran Council (1512–17): Studies on its Membership, Diplomacy and Proposals for Reform*. Aldershot, Hants.: Variorum, 1993. [A collection of previously published articles.]

Mullett, Michael A. *The Catholic Reformation*. London; New York: Routledge, 1999.

O'Connell, Marvin R. *The Counter Reformation, 1559–1610*. The Rise of Modern Europe. New York: Harper & Row, 1974.

Olin. See *The Catholic Reformation: Savonarola to Ignatius Loyola*.

O'Malley, John W., ed. *Catholicism in Early Modern History: A Guide to Research*. Reformation Guides to Research 2. St Louis, Mo.: Center for Reformation Research, 1988.

—. *Trent and All That: Renaming Catholicism in the Early Modern Era*. Cambridge, Mass.: Harvard University Press, 2000.

Pastor, Ludwig von. *The History of the Popes: From the Close of the Middle Ages, Drawn from the Secret Archives of the Vatican and other Original Sources*, ed. and trans. F.I. Antrobus, R.F. Kerr, E. Graf, OSB, and E.F. Peeler. 41 vols. London; St Louis, Mo.: K. Paul, Trench, Trubner; Routledge & K. Paul; Herder [imprint varies], 1891–1961. [Originally published as *Geschichte der Päpste seit dem Ausgang des Mittelalters, mit Benutzung des päpstlichen Geheim-archives und vieler anderer Archive*. 16 vols. in 21. Freiburg-im-Breisgau: Herder, 1886–1933.]

Renaudet, Augustin. *Préréforme et humanisme à Paris pendant les premières guerres d'Italie (1494–1517)*. Collection d'études d'histoire littéraire et de linguistique 6. Bibliothèque elzévirienne, n.s.:

Études et documents. Paris: Champion, 1916. 2nd ed. Paris: Librairie d'Argences, 1953.

Venard, Marc. "Réforme, Réformation, Préréforme, Contre-Réforme... Étude de vocabulaire chez les historiens récents de langue française." In *Historiographie de la Réforme*, ed. Philippe Joutard. Neuchâtel; Paris: Delachaux & Niestlé, 1977. [Reprinted in Venard's *Le catholicisme à l'épreuve dans la France du XVIe siècle* (Paris: Cerf, 2000), pp. 9–26. A collection of thirteen of his previously published articles, with a new article, "Rétrospection."]

—. *Histoire du christianisme, des origines à nos jours*. Vol. 8: *Le temps des confessions (1530–1620/30)*. Ed. Jean-Marie Mayeur. Paris: Desclée-Fayard, 1992.

General Bibliography

This General Bibliography lists the sources which document specific or particular topics treated in the book. For sources of wider scope or which contain English translations of sources, see the preceding Select Bibliography.

Alberigo, Giuseppe. "The Reform of the Episcopate in the *Libellus* to Leo X by the Camaldolese Hermits Vincenzo Querini and Tommaso Giustiniani." In *Reforming the Church Before Modernity: Patterns, Problems and Approaches*, ed. Christopher M. Bellitto and Louis I. Hamilton, pp. 139–52. Church, Faith and Culture in the Medieval West. Aldershot, Hants.; Burlington, Vt.: Ashgate, 2005.

Annaert, Philippe. *Les collèges au féminin: Les Ursulines; Enseignement et vie consacrée aux XVIIe et XVIIIe siècles.* Collection VC 3. Namur: Vie consacrée, 1992.

Annales Camaldulenses ordinis Sancti Benedicti ... , ed. Giovanni Benedetto Mittarelli and Anselmo Costadoni. 9 vols. Venice, 1755–1773. Repr. Farnborough, Hants.: Gregg, 1970.

Audisio, Gabriel. *Les Français d'hier.* Vol. 2: *Des croyants, XVe–XIXe siècle.* Paris: Armand Colin, 1996.

Augustijn, Cornelis. *Erasmus: His Life, Works, and Influence.* Trans. J.C. Grayson. Toronto; Buffalo: University of Toronto Press, 1991.

Bedouelle, Guy. *Lefèvre d'Étaples et l'intelligence des Écritures.* Travaux d'humanisme et Renaissance 152. Geneva: Droz, 1976.

—. *Le Quincuplex psalterium de Lefèvre d'Étaples: Un guide de lecture.* Travaux d'humanisme et Renaissance 171. Geneva: Droz, 1979.

— and Bernard Roussel. *Le temps des Réformes et la Bible.* La Bible de tous les temps 5. Paris: Beauchesne, 1989.

Bellarmine, Robert. *De potestate summi pontificis in rebus temporalibus.* Rome, 1610. [English translation: *Power of the Pope in temporal affairs, against William Barclay.* Ed. and trans. George Albert Moore. The Moore Series of English Translations of Source Books. Chevy Chase, Md.: Country Dollar Press, 1949.]

—. *Disputationum* [*Roberti Bellarmini*] *de controversiis christianae fidei adversus huius temporis haereticos* [*epitome*]. 3 vols. Ingolstadt: Sartorii, 1586–1593. Repr. Cologne: Bernhard Walter, 1619–1620; many later editions.

Bentley, Jerry H. *Humanists and Holy Writ: New Testament Scholarship in the Renaissance*. Princeton, N.J.: Princeton University Press, 1983.

Bergin, Joseph. *The Making of the French Episcopate, 1589–1661*. New Haven: Yale University Press, 1996.

Bernhard, Jean, Charles Lefebvre, and François Rapp. *L'Époque de la Réforme et du concile de Trente*. Histoire du droit et des institutions de l'Église en Occident 14. Paris: Cujas, 1989.

Bonnefoy, Yves. *Rome, 1630: L'horizon du premier baroque, suivi de Un des siècles du culte des images*. Idées et recherches. Paris: Flammarion, 1994. Repr. 2000. [First part originally published 1970; second part originally published 1989.]

The Book of Concord: The Confessions of the Evangelical Lutheran Church. Ed. Robert Kolb and Timothy J. Wengert. Trans. Charles Arand et al. Minneapolis: Fortress Press, 2000.

Borromeo, Charles. *Acta Ecclesiae Mediolanensis*. Milan: Pacificum Pontium, 1582.

Borromeo, Federico. *De pictura sacra*. Milan, 1624. [Italian edition: *Della pittura sacra*, ed. B. Agosti. Quaderni del Seminario di storia della critica d'arte 4. Pisa: Scuola normale superiore di Pisa, 1994.]

Bosio, Antonio. *Roma sotterranea*. Rome: Facciotti, 1632 [*sic*, 1635]. Repr. Rome: Edizioni Quasar, 1998.

Bradshaw, Brendan, and Eamon Duffy, eds. *Humanism, Reform, and the Reformation: The Career of Bishop John Fisher*. Cambridge; New York: Cambridge University Press, 1989.

Bricci, Giovanni. *Relatione sommaria del solenne apparato e cerimonia ... per la canonizatione de gloriosi santi Isidore di Madrid, Ignatio di Loiola, Francesco Xaueria, Teresa di Giesu, e Filippo Nerio Fiorentino ...* . Rome: Andrea Fei; Naples: Per Secondino Roncagliolo, 1622.

Briçonnet, Guillaume, and Marguerite d'Angoulême. *Correspondance, 1521–1524*. Ed. Christine Martineau and Michel Veissière, with the assistance of Henry Heller. 2 vols. Travaux d'humanisme et Renaissance 141, 173. Geneva: Droz, 1975–1979.

Brockey, Liam Matthew. *Journey to the East: The Jesuit Mission to China, 1579–1724*. Cambridge, Mass.: Harvard University Press, 2007.

Bullarum privilegiorum ac diplomatum Romanorum pontificum amplissima collectio. Ed. Charles Cocquelines. 14 vols. in 28. Rome: Typis S. Michaelis ad Ripam, 1739–1844.

Cajetan [Tommaso de Vio]. *Cajetan Responds: A Reader in Reformation Controversy*. Ed. and trans. Jared Wicks. Washington, D.C.: The Catholic University of America Press, 1978.

Calvin, John. *Opera selecta*. Ed. Petrus Barth, Dora Scheuner, and Wilhelm Niesel. 5 vols. Munich: Christoph Kaiser, 1926–1963.

Cantimori, Delio. *Eretici italiani del Cinquecento e altri scritti*. Ed. Adriano Prosperi. Biblioteca di cultura storica 193. Turin: Einaudi, 1992.

—. *Eretici italiani del Cinquecento e Prospettive di storia ereticale italiana del Cinquecento*. Ed. Adriano Prosperi. Turin: Einaudi, 2002.

Catechism of the Council of Trent for Parish Priests, issued by Order of Pope Pius V. Ed. and trans. John A. McHugh, OP, and Charles J. Callan, OP. New York: Joseph Wagner; London: Herder, 1923. [Many reprints.]

Catechismus romanus, seu, Catechismus ex decreto Concilii tridentini ad parochos Pii Quinti pont. max. iussu editus. Ed. Pedro Rodriguez and Ildefonso Adeva. Città del Vaticano: Libreria Editrice Vaticana; Navarra: Universidad de Navarra, 1989. [Originally published as *Catechismus ex decreto Concilii tridentini ad parochos Pii Quinti pont. max. iussu editus*. Rome: In aedibus Populi Romani apud Paulum Manutium, 1582.]

Catherine of Siena. *The Dialogue*. Trans. Suzanne Noffke, OP. Classics of Western Spirituality. New York: Paulist Press, 1980.

Chaline, Olivier. *La reconquête catholique de l'Europe centrale, XVIe–XVIIIe siècle*. Paris: Cerf, 1998.

Charles de Genève. *Les Trophées sacrés, ou missions des Capucins en Savoie … .* Ed. Félix Tisserand. 3 vols. Mémoires et documents publiés par la Société d'histoire de la Suisse romande, series 3,

12–14. Lausanne: Tisserand, 1976. [The text dates from the seventeenth century.]

Châtellier, Louis. *The Europe of the Devout: The Catholic Reformation and the Formation of a New Society*. Trans. Jean Birrell. Past and present publications. Cambridge; New York: Cambridge University Press; Paris: Éditions de la Maison des sciences de l'homme, 1989. [Originally published as *L'Europe des dévots*. Nouvelle bibliothèque scientifique. Paris: Flammarion, 1987.]

Collett, Barry. *Italian Benedictine Scholars and the Reformation: The Congregation of Santa Giustina of Padua*. Oxford Historical Monographs. Oxford: Clarendon Press; New York: Oxford University Press, 1985.

Congar, Yves. *Vraie et fausse réforme dans l'Église*. Unam Sanctam 72. Paris: Cerf, 1950. 2nd ed. 1968.

Coster, Franz. *Libellus sodalitatis, hoc est, Christianarum institutionum libri quinque, in gratiam sodalitatis B. Virginis Mariae*. Antwerp: Plantin Press; Ingolstadt: Sartorii, 1586. [Many reprints.]

Decreta prouincialis concilii Senonensis ... . Paris: Simon de Colines and Guillaume Davoust, 1529.

Deutsche Reichstagsakten unter Kaiser Karl V. Vol. 3. Ed. Adolf Wrede. Gotha: Andreas Perthes, 1901. Repr. Göttingen: Vandenhoeck & Ruprecht, 1965.

Dompnier, Bernard. *Le venin de l'hérésie: Image du protestantisme et combat catholique au XVIIe siècle*. Chrétiens dans l'histoire. Paris: Le Centurion, 1985.

Ducornet, Étienne. *Matteo Ricci, le lettré d'Occident*. Epiphanie; Histoire. Paris: Cerf, 1992.

Dupront, Alphonse. *Genèses des temps modernes: Rome, les Réformes et le Nouveau Monde*. Ed. Dominique Julia and Philippe Boutry. Hautes études. Paris: Gallimard; Seuil, 2001.

—. *Le mythe de croisade*. 4 vols. Bibliothèque des histoires. Paris: Gallimard, 1997.

Dussel, Enrique D. *A History of the Church in Latin America: Colonialism to Liberation (1492–1979)*. Trans. and revised by Alan Neely. Grand Rapids, Mich.: Eerdmans, 1981.

—. *Les évêques hispano-américains, défenseurs et évangélisateurs de l'Indien, 1504–1620*. Veröffentlichungen des Instituts für Europäische Geschichte Mainz 58. Abteilung Abendländische Religionsgeschichte. Wiesbaden: Steiner, 1970.

Erasmus. *Collected Works of Erasmus*. Vol. 66: *Spiritualia*. Ed. John W. O'Malley. Ed. and trans. Charles Fantazzi, Erika Rummel, and Jennifer Tolbert Roberts. Toronto: University of Toronto Press, 1988.

Étiemble [René]. *Les Jésuites en Chine (1552–1773): La querelle des rites*. Collection archives 25. Paris: R. Julliard, 1966.

Farge, James K. *Biographical Register of Paris Doctors of Theology, 1500–1536*. Subsidia Mediaevalia 10. Toronto: Pontifical Institute of Mediaeval Studies, 1980.

—. *Orthodoxy and Reform in Early Reformation France: The Faculty of Theology of Paris, 1500–1543*. Studies in Medieval and Reformation Thought 32. Leiden: Brill, 1985.

Febvre, Lucien. "Idée d'une recherche d'histoire comparée: Le cas Briçonnet." *Annuaire de l'École pratique des hautes études*. Paris, 1946. Reprinted in his *Au coeur religieux du XVIe siècle*, pp. 145–63. Bibliothèque générale de l'école pratique des hautes études 6. Paris: S.E.V.P.E.N., 1957. 2nd ed. 1968. Repr. 1983.

Fisher, John. *The English Works of John Fisher, Bishop of Rochester: Sermons and Other Writings, 1520 to 1535*. Ed. Cecilia A. Hatt. Oxford; New York: Oxford University Press, 2002.

—. *The English Works of John Fisher*. Ed. John E.B. Mayor. Early English Text Society, Extra Series, 27. London: Trübner, 1876. Repr. Millwood, N.Y.: Kraus, 1976.

Ganoczy, Alexandre. *Le jeune Calvin: Genèse et évolution de sa vocation réformatrice*. Veröffentlichungen des Instituts für Europäische Geschichte Mainz 40. Abteilung Abendländische Religionsgeschichte. Wiesbaden: Steiner, 1966.

Gerson, Jean. *Oeuvres complètes*. Ed. Palémon Glorieux. 10 vols. Paris: Desclée, 1960–.

Gleason, Elisabeth G. *Gasparo Contarini: Venice, Rome, and Reform*. Berkeley: University of California Press, 1993.

Grisar, Hartmann, SJ, ed. *Jacobi Laínez Disputationes tridentinae ad manuscriptorum fidem edidit et commentariis historicis instru-*

xit. Vol. 1: *Disputatio de origine jurisdictionis episcoporum et de romani pontificis primatu*. Innsbruck: Rauch; Regensburg: Pustet, 1886.

Halecki, Oscar. *From Florence to Brest (1439–1596)*. Rome: Sacrum Poloniae Millennium; New York: Fordham University Press, 1958. Repr. North Haven, Conn.: Archon Books, 1968.

Hanke, Lewis. *Bartolomé de las Casas: An Interpretation of his Life and Writings*. The Hague: Martinus Nijhoff, 1951.

—. *The Spanish Struggle for Justice in the Conquest of America*. Philadelphia: University of Pennsylvania Press, 1949.

Heers, Jacques. *Le Moyen âge, une imposture*. Collection Vérités et légendes. Paris: Perrin, 1992.

Index des livres interdits. Ed. J.M. De Bujanda et al. 11 vols. Sherbrooke, Québec: Centre d'Études de la Renaissance, Éditions de l'Université de Sherbrooke; Geneva: Droz, 1984–2002. [See especially vol. 8: *Index de Rome, 1557, 1559, 1564: Les premiers index romains et l'index du Concile de Trente*.]

Jedin, Hubert. *L'évêque dans la tradition pastorale du XVIe siècle*, trans. and extended by Paul Broutin, SJ. Museum Lessianum: Section historique 16. Bruges: Desclée de Brouwer, 1953. [Originally published as "Das Bischofsideal der Katholischen Reformation." In *Sacramentum Ordinis: geschichtliche und systematische Beiträge*. Breslau: Verlag des Schlesischen Bonifatiusvereins-Blattes, 1942.]

—. *Papal legate at the Council of Trent, Cardinal Seripando*. Trans. Frederic C. Eckhoff. St Louis, Mo.: Herder, 1947. [Originally published as *Girolamo Seripando: Sein Leben und Denken im Geisteskampf des 16. Jahrhunderts*. 2 vols. Cassiciacum 2–3. Würzburg: Rita-Verlag, 1937. 2nd ed. Würzburg: Augustinus Verlag, 1984.]

Jungmann, Joseph H. *The Mass of the Roman Rite: Its Origins and Development (Missarum sollemnia)*. Trans. Francis A. Brunner. 2 vols. New York: Benziger Bros., 1951–1955. Repr. Westminster, Md.: Christian Classics, 1986.

Koop, Karl, ed. *Confessions of Faith in the Anabaptist Tradition, 1527–1660*. Trans. Cornelius J. Dyck et al. Classics of the Radical

Reformation 11. Kitchener, Ont.: Pandora Press; Scottdale, Pa.: Herald Press, 2006.

Labrot, Gérard. *L'image de Rome: Une arme pour la Contre-Réforme, 1534–1677.* Époques. Seyssel (Haute-Savoie): Champ Vallon; Paris: diffusion Presses universitaires de France, 1987.

Lactantius. *Divine Institutes.* Ed. and trans. Anthony Bowen and Peter Garnsey. Translated texts for historians 40. Liverpool: Liverpool University Press, 2003.

Ladner, Gerhart B. *The Idea of Reform: Its Impact on Christian Thought and Action in the Age of the Fathers.* Cambridge, Mass.: Harvard University Press, 1959.

Lebrun, François. *Être chrétien en France sous l'Ancien Régime, 1516–1790.* Être chrétien en France 2. Paris: Seuil, 1996.

Lecler, Joseph, SJ. *Histoire des conciles oecuméniques.* Vol. 8: *Vienne.* Paris: Orante, 1964.

—, Henri Holstein, SJ, Pierre Adnès, SJ, and Charles Lefebvre. *Histoire des conciles oecuméniques.* Vol. 11: *Trente.* Paris: Orante, 1981. [A continuation of *Histoire des conciles oecuméniques* vol. 10: *Latran V et Trente.*]

Le Gall, Jean-Marie. *Les moines au temps des réformes: France, 1480–1560.* Époques. Seyssel (Haute-Savoie): Champ Vallon, 2001.

Lemaître, Nicole. *Saint Pie V.* Paris: Fayard, 1994.

Luther, Martin. *D. Martin Luthers Werke: Kritische Gesamtausgabe* [Weimarer Ausgabe], ed. J.K.F. Knaake et al. 72 vols. in 119. Weimar: H. Böhlau, 1883–; repr. Weimar: H. Böhlau; Graz: Akademische Druck- u. Verlagsanstalt, 1964–. [Some vols. are a reprint of the 1883 ed.] [= WA, for Weimarer Ausgabe.]

—. *D. Martin Luthers Werke: Briefwechsel.* 18 vols. Weimar: H. Böhlau, 1930–1985; repr. of early vols. 1969. [Part 4 of *D. Martin Luthers Werke: Kritische Gesamtausgabe.*]

—. *Luther's Works,* ed. Jaroslav Pelikan and Helmut T. Lehmann. 55 vols. St Louis, Mo.: Concordia Publishing House; Philadelphia: Fortress Press, 1955–1986. [=*LW*.]

Maritain, Jacques. *On the Church of Christ: The Person of the Church and Her Personnel.* Trans. Joseph W. Evans. Notre Dame, Ind.: University of Notre Dame Press, 1973. [Originally published as *De l'Église du Christ: La personne de l'Église et son personnel.* Paris; Bruges: Desclée de Brouwer, 1970.]

Martin, Victor. *Le Gallicanisme et la réforme catholique; essai historique sur l'introduction en France des décrets du Concile de Trente (1563–1615).* Paris: Picard, 1919.

Massaut, Jean-Pierre. *Josse Clichtove, l'humanisme et la réforme du clergé.* 2 vols. Bibliothèque de la Faculté de philosophie et lettres de l'Université de Liège 183. Paris: Belles Lettres, 1968.

Maurenbrecher, Wilhelm. Preface to *Geschichte der katholischen Reformation.* Nördlingen: Beck, 1880.

Mayer, Thomas F. *Reginald Pole: Prince and Prophet.* Cambridge: Cambridge University Press, 2000.

Minnich, Nelson H. "The Last Two Councils of the Catholic Reformation: The Influence of Lateran V on Trent," in *Early Modern Catholicism: Essays in Honour of John W. O'Malley, S.J.,* ed. Kathleen M. Comerford and Hilmar M. Pabel, pp. 3–25. Toronto; Buffalo: University of Toronto Press, 2001.

Molanus, Johannes de. *De picturis et imaginibus sacris.* Louvain: 1570; repr. Ingolstadt: 1594. [French translation: *Traité des saintes images.* Ed. and trans. François Boespflug, Olivier Christin, and Benoît Tassel. Paris: Cerf, 1996.]

Moreau, Brigitte. *Inventaire chronologique des éditions parisiennes du XVIe siècle.* Vol. 1: *1501–1510.* Histoire générale de Paris. Paris: Imprimerie municipale, 1972. [Based on the work of Philippe Renouard.]

Morgain, Stéphane-Marie. *Pierre de Bérulle et les Carmélites de France: La querelle du gouvernement, 1583–1629.* Histoire. Paris: Cerf, 1995.

Mozzarelli, Cesare and Danilo Zardin, eds. *I tempi del Concilio: Religione, cultura e società nell'Europa tridentina.* Biblioteca del Cinquecento 70. Rome: Bulzoni, 1997.

O'Malley, John W. *The First Jesuits.* Cambridge, Mass.: Harvard University Press, 1993.

Paleotti, Gabriele. *Discorso intorno alle imagini sacre et profane, diviso in cinque libri.* Bologna: Alessandro Benacci, 1582.

Pani, Giancarlo. "Un centenaire à rappeler: l'édition sixtine de la Septante," in *Théorie et pratique de l'exégèse: actes du troisième*

Colloque international sur l'histoire de l'exégèse biblique au XVIe siècle, Genève, 31 août–2 septembre 1988, ed. Irena Backus and Francis Higman, pp. 413–28. Études de philologie et d'histoire 43. Geneva: Droz, 1990.

Prodi, Paolo. "Controriforma e/o riforma cattolica: Superamento di vecchi dilemmi nei nuovi panorami storiografici." *Römische historische Mitteilungen* 31 (1989): 227–37.

Prosperi, Adriano. *Il Concilio di Trento: Una introduzione storica.* Piccola biblioteca Einaudi n.s. 117. Turin: Giulio Einaudi Editore, 2001.

Ravier, André, SJ. *Francis de Sales, Sage and Saint.* Trans. Joseph D. Bowler. San Francisco: Ignatius Press, 1988. [Originally published as *Un sage et un saint, François de Sales.* Paris: Nouvelle Cité, 1985.]

A Reformation Debate: Sadoleto's Letter to the Genevans and Calvin's Reply. Ed. John C. Olin. New York: Harper & Row, 1966. Repr. New York: Fordham University Press, 2000.

Reinhard, Wolfgang. "Pressures towards Confessionalization? Prolegomena to a Theory of the Confessional Age." In C. Scott Dixon, ed., *The German Reformation: The Essential Readings*, pp. 169–92. Blackwell Essential Readings in History. Oxford; Malden, Mass.: Blackwell, 1999. [Originally appeared as "Zwang zur Konfessionalisierung? Prolegomena zu einer Theorie des konfessionellen Zeitalters." *Zeitschrift für Historische Forschung* 10 (1983): 257–77.]

Rex, Richard. *The Theology of John Fisher.* Cambridge; New York: Cambridge University Press, 1991.

Ritter, Moriz. *Deutsche Geschichte im Zeitalter der Gegenreformation und des dreissigjährigen Krieges (1555–1648).* 3 vols. Stuttgart: Cotta, 1889–1908. 2nd ed. Darmstadt: Wissenschaftliche Buchgesellschaft, 1962.

Ruiz de Montoya, Antonio. *The Spiritual Conquest Accomplished by the Religious of the Society of Jesus in the Provinces of Paraguay, Paraná, Uruguay, and Tape.* Trans. C.J. McNaspy, John P. Leonard, and Martin E. Palmer. Jesuit Primary Sources in

English Translations, series 1, 11. St Louis, Mo.: Institute of Jesuit Sources, 1993.

Rummel, Erika, ed. *Biblical Humanism and Scholasticism in the Age of Erasmus*. Brill's Companions to the Christian Tradition 9. Leiden: Brill, 2008.

Sadoleto, Jacopo. *Opera quae exstant omnia: Quorum plura sparsim vagabantur, quaedam doctorum virorum cura nunc primum prodeunt*. 4 vols. Verona: Tumerman, 1737–1738. Repr. Ridgewood, N.J.: Gregg Press, 1964.

—. *Sadoleto on Education: A Translation of the De pueris recte instituendis*. Ed. and trans. Ernest T. Campagnac and Kenneth Forbes. London; New York: Oxford University Press, H. Milford, 1916. [Originally published as *De pueris recte instituendis*. Venice: Giovanni Antonio and the Sabio Brothers for Melchior Sessa, 1533.]

Sainte-Beuve, Charles-Augustin. *Port-Royal*. Paris: E. Renduel; Hachette, 1840–1859.

Sarpi, Paolo. *Istoria del Concilio Tridentino*. London, 1619. [Modern Italian editions exist by Giovanni Gambarin, 3 vols., Scrittori d'Italia 151–3 (Bari: Guis, Laterza & Figli, 1935); Renzo Pecchioli, 2 vols. (Florence: Sansoni, 1966); and Corrado Vivanti, 2 vols., Nuova universale Einaudi 156 (Turin: Einaudi, 1974). English versions: *The Historie of the Councel of Trent: In which are declared ... the practises of the court of Rome, to hinder the Reformation of their errors, and to maintaine their greatnesse*. London: R. Barker; J. Bill, 1620. *History of Benefices; and Selections from "History of the Council of Trent."* Ed. Peter Burke. New York: Washington Square Press, 1967.]

Simoncelli, Paolo. *Evangelismo italiano del Cinquecento: Questione religiosa e nicodemismo politico*. Italia e Europa. Rome: Istituto storico italiano per l'età moderna e contemporanea, 1979.

Tacchi Venturi, Pietro. "La canonizzazione e la processione dei cinque santi negli scritti e nei disegni di due contemporanei Giovanni Bricci e Paolo Guidotti Borghese." In Comitato Romano Ispano per le Centenarie Onoranze, *La canonizzazione dei Santi Ignazio di Loiola, fondatore della Compagnia di Gesù e Francesco Saverio, apostolo dell'Oriente*. Rome: Grafia, 1922.

Tallon, Alain. *Conscience nationale et sentiment religieux en France au XVIe siècle: Essai sur la vision gallicane du monde.* Le noeud gordien. Paris: Presses universitaires de France, 2002.

—. *La France et le concile de Trente (1518–1563).* Bibliothèque des Écoles françaises d'Athènes et de Rome 295. Rome: École française de Rome; Paris: diffusion de Boccard, 1997.

—. *Le concile de Trente.* Histoire. Paris: Cerf, 2000.

Tanner, Norman P, SJ. *Decrees of the Ecumenical Councils.* 2 vols. London: Sheed & Ward; Washington, D.C.: Georgetown University Press, 1990. [= Tanner, *Decrees.*]

Teresa of Avila. *The Collected Works of St. Teresa of Avila.* Trans. Kieran Kavanaugh, OCD, and Otilio Rodriguez, OCD. 3 vols. Washington, D.C.: Institute of Carmelite Studies, 1976–1985.

Veissière, Michel. *L'évêque Guillaume Briçonnet (1470–1534): Contribution à la connaissance de la réforme catholique à la veille du Concile de Trente.* Provins (Seine-et-Marne): Société d'histoire et d'archéologie, 1986.

Venard, Marc. *Réforme protestante, réforme catholique dans la province d'Avignon au XVIe siècle.* Histoire religieuse de la France 1. Paris: Cerf, 1993.

Wanegffelen, Thierry. *Une difficile fidélité: Catholiques malgré le concile en France, XVIe–XVIIe siècles.* Histoires. Paris: Presses Universitaires de France, 1999.

Zachman, Randall C. *John Calvin as Teacher, Pastor, and Theologian: The Shape of His Writings and Thought.* Grand Rapids, Mich.: Baker Academic Press, 2006.

Zoli, Sergio. *Europa libertina tra controriforma e illuminismo: L' "Oriente" dei libertini e le origini dell'Illuminismo: studi e ricerche.* Biblioteca Cappelli. Bologna: Cappelli, 1989.

Zwingli, Huldreich. *Huldreich Zwinglis Werke* [and] *Huldrici Zwinglii Opera.* 8 vols. in 11. Zurich: Schulthess, 1828–1842.

Index of Persons

Index of Places and Subjects

texts 72 n2; liturgy 19, 87, 116–17, 132; rhetoric 19. *See also* Bible: Vulgate

Lazaristes; Vincentians 94 n7

Leipzig, Colloquy of (1534) 47

Lepanto: naval battle of 102, 130

Libellus to Pope Leo X 18–19

Libellus reformationis (1562) 83

liturgy: Byzantine 131; in Chinese 128; Latin 19, 82, 132; reforms of at Trent 86–7, 116

Louvain (Leuven): Index of Prohibited Books 58

Low Countries: sodalities in 123

Lyons: and Pagnini's Bible 53

Madrid, imperial capital 108

Manila: college of Santo Tomás 127

Mass: abuses in celebrating 43, 74; proper celebration 86, 117; and Luther 96; as sacrifice 74, 95–6

Matrimony 72, 74

Meaux (Seine-et-Marne) 52, 59, 60

Messina (Sicily): Collegio San Niccolò 57

Mexico: synods in 126

Milan: Biblioteca Ambrosiana 133 n16; *conciliabulum* 17, 20; ruled by Spain 113; Ursulines in 121

Missal, Roman (*Ordo missae*) 86

missions: in Asia 127–8; in Canada 126; in Europe 128–32; in Latin America 125–7; in parishes 118

monasticism: commendatory abbots 23; Rule 8; reform of 53–4, 120, 122; subject to bishops 19, 118

Monreale (Sicily) 115

Monti di pietà 22

Moscow: patriarchate 130

nepotism 39, 71, 83, 99, 104, 112–13, 115

nuncios 90–1, 93, 110, 113–14, 129, 130

Nuremberg, Diet of (1523) 37–8

Oratory, Congregation of: in France 94 n8; in Rome 108, 121

original sin 48, 70, 73, 95

Ottoman Empire 128, 129. *See also* Turks

Padua: abbey of Santa Giustina 54; and Francis de Sales 106; and Pomponazzi 24

paideia: as educational ideal 23–4

papacy; popes: Anabaptist critique 35; in Avignon 14–15; Calvin's critique 34; and conciliarism 16, 18; critique of in *Consilium* 41–3;

defender of the faith 102;
and dispensations 42, 45,
78, 99; divine institution
42, 65; and ecumenical colloquies 47; and Holy Years
111; and Lateran V 17–20;
Luther's critique 31; and
nepotism 39, 71, 83, 99,
104, 112–13, 115; political
relations 14, 22, 48, 70, 71,
113–14, 125; power of the
keys 42; primacy 78, 82;
reform of 15, 17, 23, 26–8,
42–5; reformist aspirations
8, 14, 38–43, 100–2, 111;
temporal authority 105–6;
and Treaty of Tordesillas
125–6; and Trent 64–5, 70,
72–9, 85, 89–90, 99, 101,
110–12; as vicar of Christ
42. *See also* Index of Persons: Adrian VI; Alexander
VI; Boniface VIII; Clement
V; Clement VII; Clement
VIII; Gregory VII; Gregory
IX; Gregory XI; Gregory
XIII; Gregory XIV; Gregory
XV; Innocent III; John
XXIII; Julius II; Julius III;
Leo X; Marcellus II; Paul
III; Paul IV; Paul V; Pius
IV; Pius V; Sixtus IV;
Sixtus V; Urban VIII
Papal States 88, 90
pardons 89, 91
Paris 52, 53; Collège de Cler-
mont 123; Council of Sens

convened in 61; Index of
Prohibited Books 58; Loyola
at 55; Montaigu college 54;
Montmartre 55; Parlement
of 54, 60; Port-Royal 121;
Ste-Geneviève abbey 119;
S.-Germain-des-Prés abbey
54, 60; S.-Jacques priory
53, 60; University and
Faculties of 54, 60
Peace of Augsburg (1555) 128
Peasants' War 39
Penance 28, 29, 71, 73, 96, 120
Philippines: missions in 127
pietas (piety): and Calvin 32–
3; as way of life 9, 23–4,
27, 106, 124
pilgrimage 18, 101
Pisa: *conciliabulum* 17, 20
plague: fear of 70
Poissy, Colloquy of (1561) 50
Polish-Lithuanian Confed-
eration 130
pope; popes: *see* papacy
Portugal: control of Brazil
125–6; episcopal choices
115; seminary in Braga 93
Prague 135; abbey of Strahov
130; Catholic conversion
130
Prato: Dominican convent in
121
preaching; sermons 50, 73;
and Briçonnet 60–1; and
Calvin 32–3; Capuchins
and 119; and Contarini 50;
and Erasmus 52; and